America's Treasures at Bayou Bend:
Celebrating Fifty Years

Fifty Years

BB

BAYOU BEND
COLLECTION AND GARDENS

America's Treasures at Bayou Bend:
Celebrating Fifty Years

MICHAEL K. BROWN

Introduction by Jonathan Leo Fairbanks
With contributions by Emily Ballew Neff

Photographs by Miguel Flores-Vianna

SCALA PUBLISHERS

in association with

THE MUSEUM OF FINE ARTS, HOUSTON

SCALA

First published in 2007 by
Scala Publishers Ltd.
Northburgh House
10 Northburgh Street
London ECIV OAT
www.scalapublishers.com

In association with The Museum of Fine Arts, Houston
P.O. Box 6826
Houston, Texas 77265-6826
www.mfah.org

ISBN-13: 978-1-85759-485-0
ISBN-10: 1-85759-485-1

Library of Congress Cataloguing-in-Publication Data available upon request

Edited by Christine Waller Manca
Designed by Phenon Finley-Smiley
Produced by Scala Publishers Ltd.
Editor, Scala Publishers: Sarah Peacock
Index by Joan Dearnley
Printed and bound in Singapore
10 9 8 7 6 5 4 3 2 1

Jacket illustrations (Front): *New York. Sofa. 1810–30. Mahogany; ash, cherry, eastern white pine,
and mahogany. The Bayou Bend Collection, gift of the Theta Charity Antiques Show, B.78.79 (cat. 70).
Photograph by Thomas R. DuBrock.*

(Back): *Bayou Bend, Philadelphia Hall.*

Half-title frontispiece and page xiv (detail): *Robert C. Joy (American, 1910–1993).
Miss Ima Hogg. 1971. Oil on canvas. 36 1/8 x 28 3/4 inches (91.8 x 73.0 cm).
The Bayou Bend Collection, gift of Miss Ima Hogg, B.71.132. Photograph by Thomas R. DuBrock.*

Main frontispiece: *Bayou Bend, north facade. Photograph by Rick Gardner.*

Pages x, xii, and 2: *Details from the wallcovering in Bayou Bend's Dining Room,
painted by William A. Mackay in oil and gold leaf on canvas, 1928.*

GENEROUS FUNDING FOR THIS PUBLICATION IS PROVIDED BY:

The Americana Foundation

The William S. and Lora Jean Kilroy Foundation

Dr. and Mrs. G. Walter McReynolds
in honor of Mrs. Mary Frances Bowles Couper

Theta Charity Antiques Show

NOTES TO THE READER

All objects are from the Bayou Bend Collection,
the Museum of Fine Arts, Houston.

Catalogue entries are by Michael K. Brown, except for those
ending with the initials EBN, which indicate that the entry is
by Emily Ballew Neff.

Each entry is preceded by an indication of whether the object
is the gift of Miss Ima Hogg or another donor:

 denotes objects given by Miss Ima Hogg.

 denotes objects given by other donors.

Contents

FOREWORD

This publication celebrates an outstanding collection and the special people who have contributed to its increasing excellence each year. It is a collection that, although begun by one woman in 1920, has been continually enriched by the generosity of others over the last five decades. The book also commemorates the fiftieth anniversary of an extraordinary act of philanthropy by Miss Ima Hogg (1882–1975): the donation of her residence, Bayou Bend, to the Museum of Fine Arts, Houston. Bayou Bend, a 1920s mansion situated within fourteen acres of gardens and woodlands, houses one of the finest collections of pre-1876 American art and antiques in the country, a collection begun by Miss Hogg in 1920 and passionately nurtured by her until her death in 1975.

This book recognizes those who, from the time of Miss Hogg's gift of Bayou Bend to the museum in 1957, have quietly and lovingly continued to support her vision of building an evermore significant collection of early American decorative arts and paintings in Houston. Miss Hogg's gifts to the Bayou Bend Collection numbered approximately 4,500 at her death. To date, more than 1,700 additional works have been acquired, thanks to the heartfelt philanthropy of hundreds of people throughout the years. As a historic house museum, Bayou Bend presents the collection in room settings that preclude the use of identification labels, as one would find on walls or by objects in a traditional museum. These circumstances make it difficult for visitors to realize that the collection they are viewing continues to change and grow each year, and that it is the wonderful result of not only Miss Hogg's philanthropy, but the generosity of many other people as well.

The symbolism of the fiftieth anniversary presented us a fortuitous way to shape the format of the book. One hundred masterpieces have been selected to illustrate the quality, variety, and beauty of the Bayou Bend collection—fifty works given by Ima Hogg, and fifty works made possible by others. Miss Hogg firmly believed that Bayou Bend should continue to grow, to be enriched and refined, with better examples replacing lesser ones as opportunities arose. She trusted that others who shared her passion for preserving America's early material culture—and who cherished Bayou Bend as she did—would provide the dedication and support necessary to carry forth her vision. She would no doubt be pleased and humbled by the ongoing generosity of the many individuals, organizations, foundations, and corporations that have participated over the years. On pages xiv–xviii, we have endeavored to list every endowment fund, every entity, and every person who has given or supported an acquisition for Bayou Bend. Comprehensive lists like this are nearly impossible to accomplish without error, and we ask that anyone not listed, or listed incorrectly, understand that the oversight was unintended.

To celebrate the fiftieth anniversary of the gift of Bayou Bend, we share with you not only treasures from the collection, but also the fascinating, behind-the-scenes story of the development of the collection, beginning in 1920 and continuing to the present day. The introduction by Jonathan Leo Fairbanks, the Katharine Lane Weems Curator of American Decorative Arts and Sculpture, Emeritus, at the Museum of Fine Arts, Boston, and the essay by Michael K. Brown, curator of the Bayou Bend Collection, provide interesting and new contexts, which enrich our appreciation of an assemblage that today ranks as one of the world's top six collections of American art and antiques. The entries, accompanied by beautiful photographs— works of art themselves, by the talented Miguel Flores-Vianna—are intentionally brief and at times whimsical, perhaps sharing an anecdote about how an item came to be acquired, or what makes a work of art especially rare or fine. These objects are treasures and they require few words to be recognized as such—the beauty and quality is clear without words of justification. Readers interested in a catalogue of the collection are referred to the scholarly publication *American Decorative Arts and Paintings in the Bayou Bend Collection* (Princeton University Press in association with the Museum of Fine Arts, Houston, 1998).

We are most grateful to the generous sponsors of this publication: The Americana Foundation; the William S. and Lora Jean Kilroy Foundation; Dr. and Mrs. G. Walter McReynolds in honor of Mrs. Mary Frances Bowles Couper; and the Theta Charity Antiques Show. Their special support has brought to fruition this lasting tribute to those who have helped and continue to help enrich the Bayou Bend Collection. We thank Scala Publishers for publishing this book in association with the Museum of Fine Arts, Houston.

Our special thanks to the authors of *America's Treasures at Bayou Bend: Celebrating Fifty Years*: Michael K. Brown, curator of the Bayou Bend Collection; Emily Ballew Neff, curator of American painting and sculpture at the Museum of Fine Arts, Houston; and the wonderful Jonathan Fairbanks, who has shared some of his special reminiscences of Miss Ima Hogg and has placed Bayou Bend in a national context.

Their contributions to this anniversary publication reflect the respect and gratitude that all those associated with the museum and Bayou Bend feel for everyone who has helped to build, shape, preserve, and share the collection with the public. Michael Brown's essay provides an admirable overview of the leading organizations, foundations, endowments, and special individuals involved, including the extraordinary decades-long support provided by the Theta Charity Antiques Show and Houston

Junior Woman's Club. The Bayou Bend Docent Organization has not only provided more than forty years of continuous and renowned service to the museum, but also supports new accessions through its own endowment fund. The River Oaks Garden Club deserves special recognition for more than four decades of award-winning supervision of Bayou Bend's gardens and woodlands, which has included significant financial support each year. This book focuses on the collection inside the house; readers are encouraged to peruse *Bayou Bend Gardens: A Southern Oasis* (Scala Publishers in association with the Museum of Fine Arts, Houston, 2006), which celebrates the gardens and collection outside the house, for Miss Hogg was in a sense as passionate about gathering camellia and azalea varieties as she was about collecting furniture and art.

An anniversary is a time of reflection, a time to celebrate the past and look forward to the future. Please join us in a fiftieth anniversary toast to Miss Ima Hogg and all those who continue her passion for collecting great works of art for Bayou Bend and sharing them with the public. Thanks to their generosity and vision, Bayou Bend has become Houston's home for America's treasures.

Peter C. Marzio
Director
The Museum of Fine Arts, Houston

Bonnie A. Campbell
Director
Bayou Bend Collection and Gardens

ACKNOWLEDGMENTS

The concept of assembling a collection of American art, such as Ima Hogg embarked upon with great aplomb in 1920, remains as remarkable and relevant for these times as it was almost a century ago. Today the collection at Bayou Bend is internationally recognized for its superb quality, breadth, and depth—as well as for the magnificence of its physical setting in John Staub's 1928 "Latin Colonial" mansion along a bend of Buffalo Bayou. The objects that have been assembled there engage visitors' intellect while delighting their aesthetic sensibilities. This endeavor, as with every civic project that the Hogg family—Will, Ima, Mike, and his wife, Alice—undertook, whether it be in education, health care, or the arts, was always designed to benefit members of the community at large, while challenging them to participate in its ongoing development and support. As the foundation for this great institution was forged, its mission and standards of excellence were clearly defined, and they continue to guide Bayou Bend today. This publication underscores the immense worth of this vision and the public's substantive response to it over the years. Since 1957, when Ima Hogg gave Bayou Bend to the Museum of Fine Arts, Houston, more than four hundred donors have generously given objects or offered to underwrite accessions which add depth to the collection while enabling staff and docents to further its message. Today these acquisitions comprise fully a third of the collection—were it only possible to illustrate and discuss each of them in this volume! In addition to these dedicated aficionados, others have recognized the ongoing need to support operations, maintenance, and endowments for the collection, historic structures, and gardens, all directed towards enabling the institution to more fully chronicle our nation's rich artistic heritage and unique culture.

Recognizing the considerable commitment these individuals, organizations, foundations, and corporations have made, Peter C. Marzio, the director of the Museum of Fine Arts, Houston, approached members of the Bayou Bend Committee, the museum's governing body, as well as loyal friends throughout the community, with the idea of celebrating the fiftieth anniversary of Miss Hogg's gift of Bayou Bend with a handsome volume that relates the history and evolution of the collection. Their enthusiasm was immediate, and ever since, they have been steadfast in their support and encouragement. In particular, I would like to acknowledge Carolyn Frost Keenan, chairman of the Bayou Bend Committee; Isabel B. Wilson, chairman of the Board of Trustees of the Museum of Fine Arts, Houston; and Jeanie Kilroy, Alice C. Simkins, Gloria G. Anderson, and Pam Ott, longtime Bayou Bend supporters.

Bayou Bend's dedicated staff members have contributed toward the completion of this project. Director Bonnie Campbell has given this publication her complete support and maintained a faithful interest in every phase. Steve Pine, the museum's conservator, ably responded to a broad range of inquiries and undertook specific object treatments for this volume. Kristen Wetzel, Sharon Lahey, and Daphne De La Cruz helped to assemble pertinent information, as well as to mold the manuscript into a more finished work. O. B. Dyer, Ruben Obregon, and Sally White also deserve recognition and thanks.

Emily Neff, curator of American painting and sculpture at the Museum of Fine Arts, Houston, who also oversees the paintings at Bayou Bend, prepared engaging and insightful entries with characteristic flair. Her earlier work on Will Hogg as a collector, as well as past scholarly contributions by David B. Warren, founding director emeritus of Bayou Bend,

Kate Kirkland, Natalie Kroll, Linh Dan Q. Do, Elizabeth Stillinger, and the late Alice Winchester, the legendary editor of *Antiques* magazine, have been central to crafting the collection history. Miss Winchester's successor at *Antiques*, Allison Eckardt Ledes, a longtime friend of the museum, introduced us to photographer Miguel Flores-Vianna. From his first visit to Bayou Bend he was immediately smitten by its magic, as is apparent in his beautiful compositions that are evocative of the collection's sublime setting.

Thanks go to Jonathan Fairbanks for contributing the insightful introduction to this book. Since the early 1960s, he has maintained a special relationship with the institution, advising Miss Hogg as her home was transformed from a private residence to a house museum, to training the first class of docents. As his introduction relates, he and Miss Hogg soon became fast friends, and in fact she visited him at the Museum of Fine Arts, Boston, only days before her death in 1975. As a personal aside, two years later, he hired a fresh Winterthur graduate as an assistant in his department, a position I held until accepting my present one in 1980.

Bayou Bend is a house museum within the context of a larger museum and, as such, this publication benefits from the expertise of colleagues at the Museum of Fine Arts, Houston: Gwendolyn H. Goffe, associate director, finance and administration; Paul Johnson, associate director, development and membership; and Anne Wilkes Tucker, the Gus and Lyndall Wortham Curator of Photography. Other staff include Richard Hinson, Michael Kennaugh, Jonathan Davies, Ken Mazzu, and Curtis Gannon in the preparations department; Margaret Culbertson, Jon Evans, Alice Jenkins, Amy Sullivan, and Lynn

Wexler in the museum's Hirsch Library; and, Julie Bakke, Tom DuBrock, David Aylsworth, Phyllis Hastings, and Marty Stein in the Registrar's Office. I would be remiss in not recognizing the substantive contribution made by the late Dr. A. Edward Groff in collating the collection invoices, which contributed to a more thorough appreciation of the chronology.

Another department within the museum deserves special recognition; the museum archives, with its able director Lorraine Stuart and assistant archivist Amy Scott. Without their keen interest, to say nothing of their nimble maneuvering through box after box of records, the task of compiling a history of the collection would have been far more challenging and the results not nearly as insightful. A number of other institutional archives have made significant contributions since their collections comprise the papers of collectors and curators who were friends of Miss Hogg. I owe a debt of gratitude to Donna Cooke at Colonial Williamsburg, Marjorie McNinch at the Hagley Museum, Barbara File and Matthew Thurlow at the Metropolitan Museum of Art, Polly Darnell with the Shelburne Museum, and Heather Clewell at the Winterthur Museum & Country Estate. Kandy Taylor-Hille and Jonathan Plant, colleagues at the Varner-Hogg Plantation in West Columbia, were responsive to my inquiries, and I am indebted to Jonathan for bringing to my attention Mike Hogg's role in creating that house museum. I also thank Hiram Butler for contributing his insightful reflections on Bayou Bend's Wilson pottery.

The museum's publications department, under the capable leadership of Diane P. Lovejoy, has worked hard to craft a book from the voluminous drafts and myriad images submitted. No one was better qualified to serve as editor for this project than Christine Waller Manca,

assistant publications director, who possesses a special knowledge of and fondness for the institution. Over the years she has worked on a range of Bayou Bend publications, including the 1998 catalogue of the collection and David B. Warren's *Bayou Bend Gardens: A Southern Oasis*. Graphic designer Phenon Finley-Smiley worked with museum staff and photographer Miguel Flores-Vianna to ensure that the images captured the character of the place, and created an elegant design that enhanced them. Our partners at Scala Publishers, Tim Clarke, production director; Oliver Craske, editorial director; Sarah Peacock, editorial assistant; and Jennifer Wright Norman, director of publications, have a deep appreciation for Bayou Bend's unique character and it has been a pleasure to collaborate with them on this volume.

Lastly, this publication would not have been possible were it not for the vision and generosity of Jonathan M. Thomas and the Americana Foundation; the William S. and Lora Jean Kilroy Foundation; the Theta Charity Antiques Show; and Linda and Walter McReynolds, whose gift honors Mrs. Mary Frances Bowles Couper, a devoted member of the Bayou Bend Committee. Like Miss Ima Hogg, they have long recognized the value of our nation's heritage. With enthusiasm and generosity they have lent their support to a range of projects that have enabled Bayou Bend to reach an expanded audience and introduced them to America's rich artistic and historical past.

Michael K. Brown
Curator, Bayou Bend Collection

". . . I want a few authentic, worthy things as a nucleus for our Museum, to which others, as they are inclined from time to time, may add certain essentials." Miss Ima Hogg, 1946

BAYOU BEND ENDOWMENT FUNDS FOR ACQUISITIONS

The Gloria Garic Anderson Endowment Fund
for Accessions for Bayou Bend

Bayou Bend Docent Organization Endowment Fund

Houston Junior Woman's Club Charitable Fund—
An Endowment Fund for Bayou Bend Accessions

Lora Jean Kilroy Accession Endowment

W. H. Keenan Family Endowment Fund

Marian and Speros Martel Early Americana Accessions Endowment
Fund in Honor of William S. Kilroy, Sr.

Jack R. McGregor Endowment Fund for Glass

The Pamela and David Ott American Art Accessions
Endowment Fund

The Toni and Ralph Wallingford Accessions Endowment for Bayou Bend

DONORS TO THE BAYOU BEND COLLECTION

Jerry and June Adair

John Adger

Louis K. Adler

African-American Art Advisory Association

Estate of Roger Ager

AIG American General

Mrs. Ernest Alexander

Martha and James Alexander

Edward R. Allen III

Randy Allen

Robert H. Allen

Miss Mary Allis

American Association of Interior Designers,
   Gulf Coast Chapter

Mr. and Mrs. James Anderson, Jr.

Mr. and Mrs. Thomas D. Anderson

Mrs. F. L. Andrews

Mr. and Mrs. Mark Edwin Andrews

Anonymous donors (5)

Agnes Cullen Arnold Endowment Fund,
   The Museum of Fine Arts, Houston

Mrs. Paul Arnold

Mrs. Ernst Auerbach

Mrs. Edward Babcock

Michelle and Lorne Bain Family Fund

Bequest of Mary Beth Baird

Jay Baker

Baker Botts, LLP

Mr. and Mrs. J. Michael Baldwin

Mr. and Mrs. A. Leslie Ballard, Jr.

Mr. and Mrs. A. I. Bartow

Teina Baumstone

Bayou Bend Docent Organization

Bayou Bend Provisional Docent Class of 1970

Bayou Bend Provisional Docent Class of 1981

Bayou Bend Provisional Docent Class of 1987

Bayou Bend Provisional Docent Class of 1994

Bayou Bend Provisional Docent Class of 1998

Bayou Bend Provisional Docent Class of 2002

Dwight E. Beach, Jr.

Bechtel Petroleum

Audrey Jones Beck

Allen Becker

John C. Berryman

Family and Friends of Eveline Biehl

Alan Blackburn

Mr. and Mrs. W. Tucker Blaine, Jr.

Mrs. David Bland

Jack S. Blanton, Jr.

Jack S. Blanton, Sr.

Mrs. Jacob Blasser

John Blocker, Jr.

Mr. and Mrs. John P. Borman, Jr.

Ronald Bourgeault

William J. Bowen

Fentress Bracewell

Mrs. Eugenie Bullitt Branch

Danny Breen

Alfredo and Celina Hellmund Brener

John B. Brent

Thomas A. Bres

Downey Bridgwater

Family and Friends of Shirley Briscoe

Mr. and Mrs. James L. Britton, Jr.

Mr. and Mrs. James L. Britton III

Mrs. Peter Brooks

Mrs. Charles R. Brown

Family and Friends of Eleanor Bardo Brown

The Brown Foundation, Inc.

Mrs. George R. Brown

Friends of Michael K. Brown in honor
   of his 25th anniversary at Bayou Bend

Dorothy Murie Bruce

Family and Friends of Marilyn Perkins Buie

Philip Burguieres

Dr. and Mrs. James J. Butler

Mrs. James Walker Cain

Dr. Royall M. Calder

Dr. and Mrs. Benjamin Caldwell, Jr.

Rogers Clark Caldwell

William R. Camp, Jr.

Bonnie A. Campbell

Mrs. Dan H. Carpenter

Ralph Carpenter

Mrs. Patricia B. Carter

Dr. C. Thomas Caskey

Mrs. E. H. Chalmers

Charlie Chambers

Evelyn Houstoun Chew

Ray Childress

Dorothy Dawes Chillman

Miss Helen Chillman

Tonia and Bob Clark

Harriet Cochran

Fielding L. Cocke

Mrs. Coleman

Thomas Coleman

Compaq Computer Corporation

Coneway Family Foundation

Peter R. Coneway

Allyson and Steve Cook

Mrs. Richard J. Costigan

Mr. and Mrs. Fred T. Couper, Jr.

Friends of Mr. and Mrs. Fred T. Couper, Jr.

Mr. and Mrs. Alan M. Craft

Craig & Tarlton, Inc.

Mr. and Mrs. B. W. Crain

Family and Friends of Curtis Croom

Harry H. Cullen, Jr.

Roy H. Cullen

Rose Cullen

Roy W. and Meredith T. Cullen

Chris Cunningham

Tom A. and Jeanne M. Cunningham

Michael W. Dale

Larry Davis

Alfred Deaton

Mr. and Mrs. G. F. deRidder

Mrs. Franklin Devine

James D. Didier

Pamela Diehl

Charles W. Duncan, Jr.

Charles W. Duncan III

John H. Duncan, Sr.

John H. Duncan, Jr.

Donnie R. Duplissey

C. Pharr Duson

M. Robert Dussler

O. B. Dyer 30th Anniversary Fund

Eagle Global Advisors

James B. Edwards

El Paso Corporation

Mark Elias

Mr. and Mrs. Robin Elverson

Mr. and Mrs. William J. Emrich

Sheldon R. Erikson

Mr. and Mrs. Junius F. Estill, Jr.

ExxonMobil

Mrs. Josephine Faber

Mrs. Albert B. Fay

Mr. and Mrs. M. S. Fellers

Fieldstone Partners, Inc.

Jerry E. Finger

Jonathan S. Finger

Marvy A. Finger

Richard B. Finger

Scott Finger

Walter G. Finger

First Interstate Bank of Texas, N. A.

Martha Fleischman

Friends of Donna Fleming

Mr. and Mrs. Northrop R. Fletcher

Richard Fluhr

Mr. and Mrs. Andrew Fossler

Joe H. Foy

Robert S. Frank

Mr. and Mrs. Russell M. Frankel

Eleanor Freed

Friends of Bayou Bend

Vernon Frost, Jr.

Rick L. Fry

Leila and Henri Gadbois

Patty and Allen Gage

Phyllis Galbraith

Mrs. Jean Forsythe Garwood

Morgan Garwood

Susan Garwood

Natalie L. Gayle

Edward Gaylord

John Gaylord

Harry Gee

Tom Gholson

Scott Gieselman

Chip Gill

Malcolm Gillis

Ginsburg & Levy, Inc.

Mrs. Melbern G. Glasscock

Mr. and Mrs. Alfred C. Glassell, Jr.

Alfred C. Glassell III

Mr. and Mrs. Oscar Glenn

Sean Gorman

Mr. and Mrs. Richard N. Gould

Richard E. Graf

Mr. and Mrs. Joe M. Green, Jr.

Mrs. James P. S. Griffith

Mrs. Robert E. Griffith

Jas A. Gundry

Arthur J. Gutman

Charlie Hall

Henry Hamman

Lee Hancock

Bequest of Tarrant Hancock

Kay and Charles Handly

Mrs. Harry Hanszen

Titus H. Harris

Mrs. Ruth Hartgraves

Friends of Betty Black Hatchett

Heitmann Foundation

Family and Friends of
    Florence Prickett Warren Hershey

Catherine Campbell Hevrdejs

Frank J. Hevrdejs

Robert Hewell

George S. Heyer, Jr.

Dr. and Mrs. Edward F. Heyne III

Hibernia Bank

William G. Higgs

William James Hill

William Hill Land & Cattle Company

Hirschl & Adler Galleries

Oveta Culp Hobby

Miss Ima Hogg

Estate of Miss Ima Hogg

Scott Holstead

Mrs. Maury White Holt

Dr. William P. Hood, Jr.

Cecily E. Horton

Mr. and Mrs. Richard A. Hosley II

Edward M. House II

Houston Junior Woman's Club

Mr. and Mrs. Ronald E. Huebsch

William E. Huvar, Jr.

Ima Hogg Ceramic Circle

Don Ison

Robert R. Ivany

Lee and Joe Jamail

Family and Friends of Aurelia Kurth Jameson

Peter K. Jameson

Mr. and Mrs. Robert D. Jameson

Family and Friends of Robert D. Jameson

Thomas G. Jameson

Jameson Fellows, 1979–2004

Mrs. Nancy Glanville Jewell

Walter E. Johnson

Friends and Colleagues of Linda Jolivet

Anne White Jones

Bequest of Elizabeth Rieke Jones

Harry Jones

Jack G. Jones

Carolyn Frost Keenan

Mr. and Mrs. W. H. Keenan

W. Howard Keenan, Jr.

Mr. and Mrs. William T. Keenan

John G. Kellogg

Mark Kelly

Dr. and Mrs. Mavis P. Kelsey

Kennedy Galleries, Inc.

Mr. and Mrs. Isaac C. Kerridge

Chris Kersey

Mr. and Mrs. William S. Kilroy

The William S. and Lora Jean Kilroy Foundation

William S. Kilroy, Jr.

Family and Friends of Robert L. King

Garrett Kobs

Mr. and Mrs. John La Duc

Mrs. William H. Lane

Mr. and Mrs. Edmund Langwith

Mrs. Max Levine

Bernard and S. Dean Levy, Inc.

Irvin L. Levy

Michael and Cate Linn

Linn Energy

Elizabeth Ann Lipscomb

Meredith J. Long

Mike Lucas

Mrs. John A. MacDonald

Miss Millie Manheim

Mr. and Mrs. James C. Marrow

David Marsh

Marian and Speros Martel Foundation, Inc.

Craig Massey

Ike Massey

Libbie Johnston Masterson

Mr. and Mrs. Harris Masterson III

Cora Hunton Maury

Gregory S. Maury, Jr.

Mr. and Mrs. Albert Maverick III

Mrs. Eugene May

Mr. and Mrs. Maurice McAshan

Family and Friends of Dr. Robert A. McClure

Eleanor Searle Whitney McCollum

Joseph D. McCord

Jack E. McGehee

Jack McGregor

Friends of Jack R. McGregor

Colletta and Don F. McMillian

D. Cal McNair

R. Cary McNair

Robert C. McNair

Bill Miller

Martha and Herbert Mills

Kenneth Moffet

Marjorie M. Moorhead

Mr. and Mrs. John Moran

S. Reed Morian

Robert Mosbacher, Sr.

Mrs. William Moulton

Alexander J. Mourot, M.D.

Mrs. C. H. Mullendore

Eric Mullins

William F. Murdy

Mr. and Mrs. George F. Murphy III

Katharine Prentis Murphy

Museum Collectors

Nantucket Travelers

Roy Needham

Nancy B. Negley

Mr. and Mrs. Hugo V. Neuhaus, Jr.

Fred M. Nevill

Robert New

Charles T. Newton, Jr.

NL Industries Foundation, Inc. of Houston

Mrs. James Nonemaker

Jay Oates, M.D.

William P. O'Connell

Maconda Brown O'Connor

Mr. Ralph O'Connor

William Oehmig

One Great Night in November, 1988

One Great Night in November, 1990

Dee S. Osborne

Chris O'Sullivan

Dr. and Mrs. David A. Ott

Mr. and Mrs. Alvin Owsley

Rachel Pabst

Jeffrey Paine

Randall M. Pais

Pan Texas Assembly

Robert G. Phillips

Sue Rowan Pittman

T. William Porter

John Poston

Mrs. Alice Pratt

Mr. and Mrs. Richard J. Price

Mr. and Mrs. Robert M. Prioleau

DONORS TO THE BAYOU BEND COLLECTION

CONTINUED

David Pustka
Anne Quirk
Mr. and Mrs. Paul Radtke
H. David Ramm
Harry Reasoner
Cliff Reckling
James Reckling
Steve Reckling
Mr. and Mrs. Fred Renaud, Jr.
Inez Winston Reymond
Mr. and Mrs. Raymond Riesen
Mr. and Mrs. Gregg Ring
River Oaks Garden Club
Corbin J. Robertson, Jr.
Family and Friends of Felide Robertson
Mr. and Mrs. Nelson Robinson
William Robinson
Mr. and Mrs. Dean L. Rockwell
Mrs. Joe G. Rollins
Mr. and Mrs. Robert P. Ross, Jr.
Mr. and Mrs. Maurice Rowan
Miss Anne Rowland
Mrs. Clarence A. Russell
Family and Friends of Frances M. Sacco
Mrs. Henry G. Safford, Sr.
Sarah Campbell Blaffer Foundation
Fayez Sarofim
Ms. Anne Schell
Barry Schneider
Scott Schwinger
George Sealy Family
Arthur Seeligson III
Settler's Hardware and Susan Neptune

Mrs. Dudley C. Sharp
Mr. and Mrs. Robert Shaw
Shell Oil Company Foundation
Eugene B. Shepherd
Phyllis M. Shepherd
Alice C. Simkins
Matthew R. Simmons
Charlotte Sittig
David B. Smith
Lester H. Smith
Sidney V. Smith
Mr. and Mrs. Steve Smith
John F. Staub
Mrs. Barbara Arnold Sterrett
Mr. and Mrs. David Stockwell
Neil Stone
Blanche and Robert Strange, Sr.
John Strawn
Mr. and Mrs. M. S. Stude
Joe Sutton
Jack Sweeney
Nick Swyka
Mr. and Mrs. J. Taft Symonds
Henri Tallichet
Blake Tartt III
H. Blake Tartt, Jr.
Mr. and Mrs. Charles W. Tate
James B. Tennant
Texaco, Inc.
Theta Charity Antiques Show
Thirteen Stars, L.L.C.
Ralph Thomas
Friends of Mrs. Joseph Thompson
Mrs. Raybourne Thompson
J. Lewis Thompson III
Tiffany & Co.
Stephen M. Trauber
Jack Trotter

Trunkline Gas Company
Bart Truxillo
Phyllis and Charles Tucker
Mr. and Mrs. Garrett R. Tucker
Langston Turner
Mrs. Lawrence J. Ullman
Francita Stuart Ulmer
George Valian
J. Virgil Waggoner
Mr. and Mrs. Ralph E. Wallingford
Colonel and Mrs. Therwin S. Walters, USAF, Ret.
Jim Ward
Mr. and Mrs. Stanley Ward
David B. Warren and Janie C. Lee
Hathaway Watson
Mrs. Frank A. Watts
Mrs. J. Watson Webb
Kane C. Weiner
Herbert C. Wells
Alice Sneed West Foundation
Mrs. Macrery B. Wheeler, Jr.
Thomas E. White
Mrs. Harry Wiess
Janet C. Williams
Mrs. James A. Wilson
Mr. and Mrs. Wallace S. Wilson
Mrs. Robert S. Winter
Gene M. Woodfin
Mrs. Newton Wray
Wunsch Americana Foundation
Helen York
Stuart Yudofsky
Keith and Claudia Zacharias
Nina and Michael Zilkha
Mr. and Mrs. R. E. Zimmerman
Mrs. Jane Zivley

Listing as of December 2006

INTRODUCTION

Miss Ima Hogg was, first, a collector of people. All who came into her circle fondly remember her. Everyone she met became friends. They offered ideas and resources which she assimilated and incorporated. She reprocessed their best ideas and added her own to obtain a unique vision of early American life as displayed through her collections assembled in the magnificent garden and architectural setting called Bayou Bend.

Miss Ima began to make this collection in 1920 through contacts with other antiquarians, museum professionals, and dealers across the continent. She was a pioneer collector with a thirst for new knowledge and a passion for new discoveries that led to acquisitions that opened windows on the history of the arts of three-dimensional design and crafts in early America. Most of her collections were obtained from the East Coast of the United States. At the same time, she maintained and honored her generational roots in Texas. Although she complained of the geographical remoteness of the fields from which she obtained collections, such distance seemed not to diminish her zeal and ability to obtain the best. There are few people today who can personally trace her many experiences with varied sources: collectors, dealers, museum curators and directors. Broader yet were her numerous friendships formed in other humanistic pursuits. These include music, horticulture, history, and architecture, to name but a few of her many interests and areas of learning. How then is it possible to adequately limn the story of this grand lady who, as former Texas governor John Connally stated, will always be the First Lady of Texas?

My entry into Miss Ima's world began indirectly in 1961 when Charles F. Montgomery, director of the Winterthur Museum in Delaware, led a group of graduate students from the Winterthur fellowship program to New York City on a field trip. We called upon the famous antiquarian John Walton, who was an outstanding dealer of early American furniture and decorative arts. John took us into the back of his shop, where he showed us an eighteenth-century American-made easy chair (cat. 39). Never before had I seen a chair that retained its original covering of flamestitch needlework. This rarity Montgomery recommended to Miss Ima Hogg, who promptly acquired it for her collection at Bayou Bend.

Montgomery then swept me into Miss Ima's vast network of friends. He knew that she was donating her home and its collections to the Museum of Fine Arts, Houston. He felt that she needed a curator. Soon to graduate, I was looking for a job. In March 1961, Miss Ima invited me to visit and stay at Bayou Bend to talk things over. During the visit, she explained that she did not think that the time was right to hire a curator. She needed to accomplish much before moving from her home. Yet a lasting friendship developed in the course of that week. I learned of the greatness of her collection and soon became a willing aid to examine items on the East Coast that she wished to consider.

On my return to Delaware, Montgomery invited me to join the Winterthur staff. No sooner had I accepted a curatorial position than Miss Ima called and asked me to start a docent-training program at Bayou Bend. She wanted me to arrive in Houston in July 1961, to present a month-long course for her first class of docents. I explained that having just been hired at Winterthur, that probably would be impractical. But I promised to ask. Understandably,

Montgomery adamantly refused my leave request. Phoning Miss Ima, I explained that with a new job, I could not now take off to teach at Bayou Bend. In a sweet voice, Miss Ima responded, "Well, we will see." Once Miss Ima decided on a course of action, few were able to divert her plans. Shortly thereafter I was called into the director's office to be informed that I was being sent to Houston on a mission to teach Miss Ima's docents who were to become the future guides for Bayou Bend. This assignment was proclaimed a professional gesture of good will.

In Houston Miss Ima asked me to present "informal" talks to the docents about the collections, room by room, every morning from nine until noon for a month. Miss Ima made certain that every word I spoke was recorded on tapes in order to produce a docent's guidebook. The following year, Miss Ima asked me to give a talk about the collections of Bayou Bend to the 1962 Williamsburg Antiques Forum. This Forum, which was regularly attended by Miss Ima, attracted important collectors from across the nation. While this lecture was not the first public notice

of Bayou Bend, it was news to many in the antiques world. The big news was that Miss Ima's collection and Bayou Bend was to become a place that would benefit the general public.

Collecting for Miss Ima seemed to be an instinctive process. Almost every collector of consequence can point to an object that formed a turning point in his or her life. Such a discovery is a moment of transcendent awareness that leads the collector into a lifetime of further discoveries. Collectors of consequence do not simply furnish a residence; they shape their understanding,

Fig. 1. *Jonathan Fairbanks (left) trained the first class of Bayou Bend docents in 1961. Miss Ima Hogg is in the center, behind the newel post. Photograph: Hickey & Robertson; The Museum of Fine Arts, Houston, Archives.*

their lives, and the lives of others by recognizing relationships among things that, for most people, have no real kinship. This is the arena where the poetic imagination of the creative collector intersects with the historic past in a search for virtual or plausible relationships between objects within comparable aesthetic or stylistic timeframes. For those who wish to represent the historic human habitat in its fullness and at its ideal best, the process is both complex and catalytic. Over time, the search becomes a seemingly endless pursuit requiring knowledge, patience, means, and longevity. Fortunately, Miss Ima enjoyed all four of these blessings.

No wonder, then, that Bayou Bend seemed forever in a state of remodeling as different collections from various times and places required installation of architectural settings. Unlike at Winterthur, where Henry Francis du Pont used period woodwork, salvaged from early buildings for his more than a hundred period rooms, Miss Ima wisely chose not to collect period interior woodwork. Instead, she devoted her energy to collecting the best furniture, furnishings, and paintings made in early America. Once a critical mass was gathered, Miss Ima could then select the best models for replica woodwork appropriate to the era and region where the furniture was made. The period room represents the most complex, technically demanding, high-maintenance problems in the sphere of museum exhibitions. The microcosmic restructuring of an imagined past with genuine period objects is not for the faint of heart or for those without deep pockets. Probably for these reasons, period room displays have fallen into some disfavor with efficiency-prone modern museums. Despite this, the period room still holds a great popular appeal among the visiting public. Simply stated, people enjoy seeing objects in their normal context of human use. The human drama of the period room is widely appealing.

A visit to Bayou Bend reveals more than twenty-five period rooms. A consideration of a

few of the ground-floor rooms suffices to grasp the texture and magnificence of all. The rooms are not arranged in chronological sequence, as the shape of the house and the circumstances of collecting posed a problem of logical "fit" for a residence. Miss Ima regarded Bayou Bend as a home with collections, not a "museum." Indeed, it is a collection of superb works of art arranged in meaningful groupings that range in time from America's seventeenth to the nineteenth centuries.

The Pine Room (illustrated on pages 34–35) was used as a library when Bayou Bend was Miss Hogg's residence. Miss Ima wondered how to maintain a modern library in this room when she did not own a collection of leather-bound period books to form the appearance of an early eighteenth-century room. I suggested that she make a curtain wall of wooden panels that could conceal her modern books and at the same time form a proper setting for her collection of early eighteenth-century furnishings. She liked that idea. In the 1960s she had the room remodeled with paneled walls. The room now serves as a setting for a handsome William and Mary style New England highboy, or chest on stand, with its vigorously figured burled veneer (cat. 10). It also contains tall-backed chairs of the period. One of these chairs I examined on behalf of Miss Ima in the New York shop of Bernard Levy. It is a caned-back chair and hence a rare specimen in American furniture history (cat. 9). Most caned-back chairs of this time were made in England rather than the American colonies. Miss Ima was aware of this fact, but was eager to obtain an exceptional American example. Since diagnostic tools of wood analysis were not sufficiently developed at the time, this was a heady assignment. I'm happy to say that the decision to make the purchase turned out to be right. It is an exceptional caned-back chair—made in the British colonies of North America.

Beyond the Pine Room is the Massachusetts Room, or Blue Room (illustrated on page 51).

In this room stands the Massachusetts wing chair with its original flamestitch upholstery that Montgomery showed his students in New York City (cat. 39). Here also is the finest collection of eighteenth-century Massachusetts furniture that one can hope to see concentrated in any collection. The double chair-back settee behind the turret top tea table (cat. 21) are both masterpieces and extreme rarities for which only a handful of comparable works survive. A set of eight side chairs matches the settee!

The Murphy Room (illustrated on pages 24–25) was named as a tribute to Katharine Prentis Murphy, a pioneer collector of Americana who was a friend of Miss Ima. Her special interest was seventeenth- and early eighteenth-century Americana, and she gave Miss Ima much encouragement. But unlike Mrs. Murphy, Miss Ima had a much broader collecting strategy. As she collected Americana throughout more than half a century of her own life, the range of styles embraced by Miss Ima vastly exceeded those of Mrs. Murphy and even in some cases beyond those of Henry Francis du Pont. In 1965, with the arrival of David Warren as curator of Bayou Bend, a massive remodeling took place to upgrade climate control and to improve and install more rooms. This included masterpieces of nineteenth-century American furniture and furnishings in rooms highlighting the Empire and Rococo Revival styles (illustrated on pages 115 and 136–37).

Miss Ima recognized the importance of including the entire panorama of the American arts up to the modern era, despite those limitations of space and means that stood in the way. In the late 1960s, when I toured Miss Ima through Winterthur, she looked at the grandeur of the Court Floor installation and exclaimed, "Oh, what I could have done had I the wherewithal of Henry Francis du Pont." But Miss Ima surpassed the achievements of Winterthur in many ways. She was not bound by the cut-off date of 1840 that determined Mr. du Pont's interests.

She installed a Texas Room (illustrated on pages 126–27) at Bayou Bend and also restored Texas buildings and collections beyond Bayou Bend. She also wisely connected her collection and its care to a distinguished urban museum, the Museum of Fine Arts, Houston, thereby ensuring Bayou Bend's relevance to a large public audience. A ceremony to dedicate Bayou Bend took place on March 5, 1966. This consummated the formal transfer of its ownership to the Museum of Fine Arts, Houston. My wife, Louisa, and I were there. It was a special event that marked a long journey of devotion that many had shared with Miss Ima. She announced that her separation from Bayou Bend was smooth and that she never felt divorced from her home. She moved to an apartment at Inwood Manor, not far distant. She reported, "Now I am free to pursue my other projects and I can watch the sunsets from my high-rise apartment."

Miss Ima pursued her interests on many fronts. In the mid-1970s she toured *Paul Revere's Boston*, one of the first exhibitions my department mounted at the Museum of Fine Arts, Boston. Five years before, I had moved from Delaware to Boston to organize the first department of American decorative arts and sculpture at that museum. I'll never forget how, as she toured the exhibition with cane in hand, she pointed to objects she liked, as well as at those that did not appeal to her. She was on her way to London on that trip. She explained that her doctor had told her not to travel, but she always made a practice of doing exactly what she wished to do. She was traveling with a companion. Despite that precaution, an accident took place: Miss Ima broke her hip while falling from a cab outside her hotel. It is reported that, from the Westminster Hospital, she called friends to inform them of the accident and the necessity of an operation. She assured those to whom she spoke that, should she not survive, they should not grieve, for she had enjoyed a full life—always doing whatever

pleased her most. She died at age 93.

Subsequent to her passing, a former staff member of my department, Michael Brown, joined Bayou Bend in 1980 to continue the important curatorial work begun by David Warren. Despite the many years that have passed, I still feel connected to Bayou Bend and to Miss Ima's desire for it to become a resource serving the greater public good—sharing its "aesthetic values, and [to] stimulate an interest in the social and economic history of our country." I suspect that Miss Ima's ever-watchful genius, wherever it may be, is trained down upon us, approving and critiquing this latest work of public record about the collections of her beloved Bayou Bend.

Jonathan Leo Fairbanks
The Katharine Lane Weems Curator of American Decorative
Arts and Sculpture, Emeritus
Museum of Fine Arts, Boston

A Bridge to the American Past, and Future:
A History of the Bayou Bend Collection

A Bridge to the American Past, and Future:
A History of the Bayou Bend Collection

From the time I acquired my first country Queen Anne armchair in 1920, I had an unaccountable compulsion to make an American collection for some Texas museum.

IMA HOGG, AUGUST 1973

Fig. 2.
Wayman Adams (American, 1883–1959).
Miss Ima Hogg. *c. 1920. Oil on canvas,*
24 1/8 x 20 1/8 inches (61.3 x 51.1 cm).
The Bayou Bend Collection, gift of Alice C. Simkins,
B.79.292.

In 1957, Miss Ima Hogg (1882–1975) transferred ownership of Bayou Bend, her home for close to three decades, to the Museum of Fine Arts, Houston. In doing so, she realized a vision she had nurtured since 1920, when she began to form a collection of early American furniture. From the very start, she had intended the collection for the public, as a means of introducing the people of Texas to the history of their country. With the donation of Bayou Bend, the home would be transformed from a private residence into a house museum to showcase the great American art she had assembled.

Miss Hogg's intent was that it be regarded as a public collection rather than as her own, and in an admirable spirit of philanthropy, she never encumbered it with restrictions. Instead, she hoped that others who shared her vision would lend their support. In 1957, as her plans came to fruition, they prompted a succession of gifts for the collection, the most prominent being the unique blue dash dish—a gift from her great friend and fellow collector Electra Havemeyer Webb (cat. 3).

Miss Hogg was inspired to acquire her first piece of early American furniture while visiting the New York portrait studio of Wayman Adams in 1920 (fig. 2). She noticed and was engaged by an eighteenth-century New England armchair. When she learned it was the product of a colonial American craftsman, her interest heightened. She perceived, in what otherwise seemed to be an unassuming object, a tangible link to the American past. It prompted her to query if, through a piece of furniture, one could explore and interpret the nation's history and culture. She shared the idea of forming a collection with her older brother, William C., known as Will (1875–1930); he not only lent his support, but readily joined his sister in this high-minded pursuit.[1]

Today, Miss Ima Hogg is most readily identified with her extraordinary collection of American paintings, furniture, and related decorative arts, but this represents only one facet of her diverse philanthropic interests. For Ima and Will Hogg, collecting was part of a more expansive plan, one designed to benefit the people of Houston and, beyond that, the citizens of their beloved Texas. The Hoggs' Progressive beliefs, which were fostered by their parents, James and Sally Stinson Hogg, define the late nineteenth-century movement to counteract the social ills that were perceived as a result of urbanization, industrialization, and immigration. James Hogg espoused this philosophy through his reform leadership as governor of Texas from 1891 to 1895. In time, the family's philanthropic causes embraced educational institutions and healthcare facilities, as well as nascent performing and visual arts organizations. In short, it was their conviction that a community's growth and prosperity required the presence of social and cultural institutions to ensure a better quality of life for its citizens.[2]

Ima and Will Hogg are identified with a group of collectors active in the period immediately following World War I who amassed some of the country's greatest assemblages of American art. In pursuing this endeavor, they relied heavily on the recognition and research of previous generations. As early as the 1780s and 1790s, a handful of individuals began to preserve objects which embodied the American past. To this first generation of antiquarians, early American pieces were largely perceived as relics or oddities; however, over time, they began to recognize these objects' value to society and reassess their meaning.[3] The mid-nineteenth century witnessed an ever-increasing regard for the significance of the national past. Scholars suggest this recognition may have been in response to dramatic changes taking place as the country's boundaries and population expanded westward, as its society began to be transformed from an agrarian culture to an industrial one, and as dissension escalated between the North and South. Ironically, the Civil War would prompt some of the earliest displays of American antiques, presented at "sanitary fairs," events organized under the auspices of the Sanitary Commission that raised funds for the Union's sick and wounded. During the 1870s, Americans celebrated a century of independence with a range of historical exhibitions held throughout the country.

By the 1890s, collectors had become more sophisticated, and they embraced an appreciation for aesthetics and craftsmanship. This broadened view was consistent with the ideals that prompted the beginnings of the Arts and Crafts movement. For many, collecting was a reaction to the dramatic changes taking place in modern American society. The earliest contributions to scholarly research in the field also appeared during this period. In 1888, John H. Buck authored *Old Plate, Ecclesiastical, Decorative, and Domestic: Its Makers and Marks.* Three years later, Irving W. Lyon published *The Colonial Furniture of New England,* and Edwin Atlee Barber's *The Pottery and Porcelain of the United States* followed in 1893. The first public collection of American decorative arts, a bequest

from Charles Leonard Pendleton, opened in 1904, at the Museum of Art, Rhode Island School of Design. The year 1906 witnessed the earliest museum exhibition of American antiques, *American Silver,* at the Museum of Fine Arts, Boston. The Metropolitan Museum of Art organized the Hudson-Fulton Exhibition in 1909; inspired by the 300th anniversary of Henry Hudson's discovery of the great river named for him, and the centennial of Robert Fulton's invention of

Fig. 3.
Ima Hogg (left) and Katharine Prentis Murphy at Bayou Bend, 1960. John Singleton Copley's Portrait of a Boy *hangs at left. Photograph: courtesy Houston Chronicle.*

Fig. 4.
Ima Hogg and Harris Masterson III at
the public dedication of Bayou Bend, March 1966.
The Museum of Fine Arts, Houston, Archives.

the steamboat, the dual exhibitions presented seventeenth-century Dutch painting and early American paintings and decorative arts.[4]

During the post-World War I years, Americans' appreciation for their historical past and artistic achievements further increased. New York emerged as the undisputed marketplace and center for scholarship in the field. During this period the Hogg siblings were often there, having taken an apartment in the city. In January 1922, *Antiques* magazine began publication, and Will ordered subscriptions for their New York and Houston addresses. Through the magazine's informative articles and advertisements, the Hoggs' knowledge of American antiques broadened, and they were kept abreast of the intricacies of the marketplace.[5] Along with *Antiques*, publications on American furniture were added to the family's voluminous library, including seminal works by Irving W. Lyon, Charles O. Cornelius, Wallace Nutting, and N. Hudson Moore.[6]

The siblings further augmented their library with auction catalogues from the American Art Association, Inc., and the Anderson Galleries. Will made extensive purchases of Windsor furniture at the Louis Guerineau Myers sale in 1921, and of early American glass at the Jacob Paxson Temple sale the following year. Despite these successes, in a letter to his sister Will questioned the auction process: "although I got excellent examples of the articles purchased, I am prone to believe that I might have done better buying from a dealer—even the favored one on Madison Avenue."[7] The results of this flurry of collecting eventually manifested themselves at Varner Plantation, the family's country house in West Columbia, approximately sixty miles south of Houston, and in their penthouse suite of offices on the eighth floor of the Armor Building in downtown Houston. In April 1920, Hogg Brothers, as the family's business interests were known, began construction of the brick-and-glass structure. The partnership, which included Miss Hogg, conducted business from this address, which housed offices for Will, Ima, and their younger brother, Mike (1885–1941). The design

of the penthouse could not have contrasted more with the building's modern exterior. Described at the time as "something new in the way of bungalows," it was as if a small white cottage had been plunked down on top of the high-rise. Its domestic character was further accentuated by being set back from the building's parapet within a landscaped roof garden. There, the early furnishings the Hoggs had collected in the East were comfortably nestled in their surroundings, hooked rugs scattered on the floor and colorful antique glass displayed in the window shelves, with the Houston skyline beyond. The penthouse interiors conformed to the Colonial Revival aesthetic that was espoused at the time, with one exception: the walls were hung with Will Hogg's collection of late nineteenth- and early twentieth-century paintings by the American master Frederic Remington, dramatic compositions capturing the conflict and clash between two cultures. Varner Plantation and the penthouse offices in the Armor Building presented the siblings an opportunity to experiment with interior spaces, and within a few years, they began to plan a residence for themselves.[8]

Throughout the 1920s, Will and Ima Hogg divided their time between Houston and New York. In addition to acquainting themselves with the auction houses and principal dealers, they also met Charles O. Cornelius, an associate curator for American art at the Metropolitan Museum of Art. Following the Hudson-Fulton exhibition, the Metropolitan had begun to form a collection of American decorative arts. Cornelius, a 1916 graduate of the Massachusetts Institute of Technology, joined the museum staff in 1917. He organized the exhibition *Furniture Masterpieces of Duncan Phyfe* in 1922, the same year it was announced that the museum had committed to the addition of a wing wholly dedicated to American architecture and decorative arts. The American Wing opened in 1924 with great fanfare.[9]

In all likelihood, the introduction of Ima and Will Hogg to Cornelius was initiated by

John Staub, a young architect who had graduated from M.I.T. in 1915, one year before Cornelius. The family had engaged Staub to work on River Oaks, the residential development they envisioned as a model of urban planning for Houston. As Hogg Brothers began to subdivide the property, a tract along Buffalo Bayou was set aside for their own residence.[10] Beginning in 1926, Staub worked closely with Miss Hogg to develop plans for the house. He was well suited for the commission; his work evinces an understanding of historical styles, and his designs are characterized by a deft handling of proportion and flow. He designed interiors largely reminiscent of their eighteenth-century predecessors, handsome spaces that would complement the Hoggs' ever-growing collection of early American furniture. One of the rooms, the library, was patterned after the Metcalf-Bowler Room, an eighteenth-century period room installed in the American Wing. Bayou Bend was completed in November 1928.[11]

The dynamic 1920s came to a vigorous conclusion, at least for Americana enthusiasts, with a landmark exhibition and two memorable sales. Between September 25 and October 9, 1929, an exhibition held to benefit the Girl Scouts of America was elegantly installed in the showrooms of the American Art Galleries (the forerunner of Sotheby's). The Girl Scout Loan Exhibition elevated American art from an antiquarian pursuit to the realm of the connoisseur and curator, and a catalogue from the exhibition found its way into Miss Hogg's library.[12] A few months earlier, in April 1929, the magnificent collection assembled by the late Howard Reifsnyder, was dispersed in the same showrooms. Reifsnyder, a successful Philadelphia wool merchant, had concentrated on mahogany masterpieces by the city's finest craftsmen. The historic sale realized $600,000, the high point occurring when Henry Francis du Pont prevailed over William Randolph Hearst to purchase the Van Pelt high chest for $44,000, a record price for American furniture at auction. Penciled comments annotated the Hoggs' copy of the Reifsnyder

catalogue, though they did not make any purchases at the sale. However, twenty-some years later, Miss Hogg acquired Reifsnyder's superb Philadelphia chest-on-chest (cat. 35). The other important sale was of the estate of Philip Flayderman of Boston, offered by the American Art Association in January 1930. Despite the unfortunate timing, only weeks after the stock market collapse, competition was as intense as it had been at the Reifsnyder auction. The top lot, a tambour desk labeled by the hitherto unknown John and Thomas Seymour of Boston, realized a staggering $30,000.

By the time of the Flayderman sale, Miss Hogg's collecting interests had deviated. A year earlier, in 1928, she purchased *Meditation (Portrait of Lorette)* by Henri Matisse, and thus began forming a collection of twentieth-century works on paper. The following summer, joining Will in Europe, she visited Paris, Munich, and Berlin, and traveled to Denmark, Sweden, and Russia. There she was captivated by contemporary European art. She purchased works by Pablo Picasso, Lyonel Feininger, Paul Klee, and Wassily Kandinsky.[13] In September, the trip came to an abrupt end, when Will died following emergency surgery in Baden Baden. Miss Hogg was devastated by the loss of her older brother, and the memory of their collecting adventures may explain her diminished interest in American furniture. During the 1930s, she redirected her time to other pursuits, such as the Child Guidance Center in Houston, which she had recently founded.[14] She became actively engaged with a succession of landscape architects in designing the extensive gardens at Bayou Bend. Her chief commitment during these years was to the Hogg Foundation for Mental Health.[15]

The dream of building a collection of American furniture for Texas, which was so aggressively pursued in the 1920s, lay dormant following the death of Will Hogg and throughout the 1930s. Ironically, it may have been the loss of her younger brother, Mike, in 1941, that prompted Miss Hogg to resume collecting.

The collection you have assembled and are keeping for us. . . is already one of the finest in the country. Certainly all of Houston is indebted to you for your vision and selectivity in making this available for our Museum.

LEE MALONE TO IMA HOGG,
JUNE 21, 1956

In 1939, Mike Hogg was invited to join a state commission charged with planning a memorial to his father in Quitman, Wood County. He had earlier been diagnosed with cancer, and as his health deteriorated he prevailed upon his sister to serve in his stead. The Governor James Stephen Hogg Memorial Shrine was created in 1941. Four years later, Miss Hogg directed her efforts and resources toward the restoration of her parents' first home, the "Honeymoon Cottage" in Quitman, which opened to the public in March 1952. Eventually she purchased her maternal grandparents' home, had it moved to the twenty-six acre park complex, and oversaw its restoration.[16]

Included in Mike Hogg's will was a provision that conveyed his interest in Varner Plantation to his sister and younger brother, Tom (1887–1949). Upon the termination of their life estates, the fifty-two acres, incorporating both house and grounds, would be conveyed to the state of Texas. The clause specified that the property would be the gift of William Clifford, Ima, Mike, and Thomas E. Hogg in memory of their parents, "in remembrance of their esteem for the pioneer of Texas, upon the condition that the State of Texas . . . shall establish within and at 'The House and Garden' a historic museum, and at and within 'The Park' a public park. . . ."[17] The timing of Mike Hogg's provision, virtually coinciding with the efforts to develop the Quitman property,

Fig. 5.
Attending the public dedication of Bayou Bend in March 1966 were Miss Hogg's sister in-law Mrs. Harry Hanszen (left) and Mrs. Hanszen's niece, Miss Alice C. Simkins. The Museum of Fine Arts, Houston, Archives.

makes clear that by the early 1940s Miss Hogg was in the process of planning for two house museums, foreshadowing the transformation of Bayou Bend.

Miss Hogg later credited Ray Dudley with the concept of converting Bayou Bend from a residence to a house museum, noting that the suggestion was made during his tenure as chairman of the Museum of Fine Arts, Houston, board in 1941–43.[18] As such, Bayou Bend would function as an adjunct to the fine arts museum, which would thereby ensure there was sufficient space to exhibit the collection and to accommodate future growth. Furthermore, the domestic interiors would define a scale and introduce settings that could not be realized in the museum galleries. While Miss Hogg had not added to the collection since 1929, this development must have reignited her interest. In 1943, she returned to New York, revisited Israel Sack, as well as Ginsburg and Levy, and returned with Rococo and classical New York chairs.

That same year, Miss Hogg presented the museum with her brother Will's renowned collection of Frederic Remington's works. A year later, in 1944, she donated to the museum the

Southwest Indian art that she had begun to assemble in the 1920s. Reminiscing about her visits to the Southwest, she related that she "discovered that the American Indian possessed a rare feeling for beauty, a fine sense of design, and superior craftsmanship." Her fascination with the culture is reflected in her collection of more than four hundred pieces of pottery, paintings, Kachina dolls, and jewelry.[19]

As Miss Hogg began to contemplate transforming Bayou Bend into a house museum, the concept had to vie for attention with a number of other obligations. To support the city during the redoubtable war years, in 1943 she was elected to a six-year term on the school board. Three years later, in 1946, she agreed to accept the presidency of the Houston Symphony. She had helped found the symphony in 1913, and she would remain intimately involved with it throughout her life.[20] Perhaps these substantive civic commitments factored into an apprehension Miss Hogg felt about resuming collecting. Furthermore, this time it was without the cajoling and encouragement of brother Will. She must have shared her concerns with James Chillman, the founding director of the Museum of Fine Arts, Houston, and a member of the faculty at Rice University. Chillman was a dear friend, as was his accomplished wife, Dorothy, who had studied interior design and taught at the Parsons School of Design in New York.

By 1946, Ima Hogg and James Chillman initiated a correspondence with Joseph Downs, Charles Cornelius's successor at the Metropolitan Museum of Art. Downs recognized what Miss Hogg was trying to achieve for the Houston museum and was generous with his time and advice. In October, she wrote him confiding her concerns:

I want again to thank you for giving so much of your precious time to discussing with me some of my collecting problems.

Having entirely abandoned the purchase of anything for so long for other preoccupations, I feel rather strange and helpless now with the growing scarcity of

American antiques and rising prices. Also, I think I am too rusty to be depending on my judgment alone. I am sure you appreciate the fact that it is a disadvantage to collect while living so far from the "market". . .

If your Board decides it will sell some of the duplicates on hand I hope you will remember us. Or, if anything comes to you for sale which you think desirable and yet cannot use, we would appreciate your referring it to the Houston Museum in care of Mr. Chillman, our Director, and in turn it will be referred to me.[21]

Downs responded to Miss Hogg's inquiry about the museum's duplicates and in February 1947 proffered a half-dozen pieces of furniture he would consider deaccessioning under this arrangement. Miss Hogg decided a Philadelphia Rococo-style dressing table and a Connecticut block-front chest-on-chest would make fitting additions. Perhaps prompted by their mutual understanding that the Metropolitan's furniture would be destined for a museum collection, she offered the dressing table to the Museum of Fine Arts, Houston, that fall, and the chest-on-chest the following year, thereby constituting the first of a succession of gifts to the Houston museum.[22]

In the decade between these initial donations to the Museum of Fine Arts and the transfer of Bayou Bend in 1957, Miss Hogg bestowed a singular group of antique furniture, numbering eighteen pieces in all and including some of the most consequential objects she would acquire. In 1950, she presented the magnificent bureau table attributed to John Townsend that she had pursued for four years and had succeeded in purchasing only a few months earlier (cat. 28). The following year, she acquired and donated the rare Boston tea table with its distinctive turreted top (cat. 21), and, in 1952, the sublime Wharton family high chest (cat. 36). Three pieces were given to the museum in 1953, including the splendid Philadelphia chest-on-chest formerly in the Reifsnyder collection (cat. 35).

A year later, she gave four more, one of them being the richly veneered, early Baroque high chest (cat. 10). The final gifts made prior to the donation of Bayou Bend were the japanned high chest (cat. 16) and the iconic Newport desk-and-bookcase (cat. 46).

In 1949, Joseph Downs resigned his position at the Metropolitan to become the founding curator of the unparalleled collection of American decorative arts that Henry Francis du Pont had assembled at Winterthur, his family's Delaware estate. Respecting his affiliation with Mr. du Pont, Miss Hogg turned to Down's successor, Vincent D. Andrus, who was likewise generous and responsive to Miss Hogg's periodic requests. In June 1953, Lee Malone, who had succeeded Chillman as the director of the Museum of Fine Arts, Houston, wrote Andrus to inquire about formalizing their relationship. Malone suggested Andrus be placed on a retainer and extended an invitation for him to visit Houston and survey Miss Hogg's collection firsthand. Francis Henry Taylor, the director of the Metropolitan, signaled his approval on Andrus's July memorandum: "Go ahead. Miss Hogg is a charmer," adding an admonition, "Houston is bloody hot at this time." This professional arrangement would last at least through 1958, but eventually lapsed, due to Andrus's health concerns.[23] In addition to examining the objects Miss Hogg was considering, Andrus would occasionally bring to her attention pieces he believed would enhance her collection, although both understood that Andrus's primary allegiance was to the Metropolitan Museum.[24]

Once Miss Hogg decided that Bayou Bend would become a house museum, she directed her attention to the placement of the furniture in a series of historical room settings. She defined her collecting priorities and began to acquire objects in other media that would complement the furniture and be appropriate for creating the desired interiors. In 1953, she started to systematically acquire American silver, pewter, and paintings. That November, she wrote Lee Malone, "As you probably know from our past conversations, it is not my intention to make a representative collection of American portraits, as surmised by Mr. Karolik. I hope someone else will, but in the meantime, if the right opportunity presents itself, I would add a few portraits as accessories, or background."[25] Nonetheless, within a year she had purchased no fewer than seven colonial portraits, including four by John Singleton Copley (cats. 31, 32, and 37), as well as Edward Hicks's beguiling *Peaceable Kingdom* (cat. 88).

Although the concept of transforming Bayou Bend into a house museum was instilled a decade earlier, by 1953 a series of developments at the Museum of Fine Arts reaffirmed the sagacity of this approach. That year, the museum announced a major gift from Miss Nina Cullinan, a trustee whose father, J. S. Cullinan, was one of the museum's original benefactors. This pledge, combined with other gifts, prompted the creation of a master plan and provided the stimulus for a series of renovations, culminating in the construction of a modern wing. Ludwig Mies van der Rohe was awarded the commission and in 1958, as his steel and glass addition was opened, so did a new chapter in the museum's history. With the addition of Cullinan Hall and Miss Hogg's gift of Bayou Bend the year before, the stature of the institution was significantly elevated.[26] Now, with the block of land the museum occupied fully committed, and the gallery spaces dedicated, the wisdom of converting Bayou Bend into a house museum was evident.

During the early 1950s, Miss Hogg formed close relationships with other principal Americana collectors, as well as a number of leading professionals. About 1951, she was introduced to Katharine Prentis Murphy (fig. 3) by Lillian Cogan, the legendary Farmington, Connecticut, antiques dealer.[27] A couple of years later, through Vincent Andrus, she became acquainted with Helen and Henry Flynt, who had created house museums in Deerfield, Massachusetts.[28] In 1953, she began to attend the Antiques Forums that had been cofounded by *Antiques* magazine and Colonial Williamsburg four years earlier. There, Miss Hogg further expanded the cadre of collectors who shared her passion and vision—the majority of them forming collections that were also destined for the public.[29] She became particularly close to Mrs. Murphy, the Flynts, as well as Ralph Carpenter, Henry Francis du Pont, Maxim Karolik, and Electra Havemeyer Webb. In addition, she became good friends with a number of professionals, including Alice Winchester, the esteemed editor of *Antiques*, John M. Graham of Colonial Williamsburg, Donald Shelley of the Henry Ford Museum, and Charles Montgomery of Winterthur. Karolik perhaps best summarized the spirit of this little band, referred to as the "Antiquees," when he wrote Miss Hogg: "When we are all together . . . I always feel that we all belong to the same family. The things we are all trying to accomplish has a meaning to each of us individually. We realize its significance, because we know where the eminent and lasting human values lie, and what they mean to the people of this nation."[30]

1957–65

I feel as if I need a great deal of advice about all the house. There are so many inconsistencies in a place like this. . . . It will simply house an American collection in what I hope will be an harmonious setting. I hope those who visit it will have a better understanding of our American heritage. That is really what it is for.

IMA HOGG TO
HENRY N. FLYNT, AUGUST 28, 1959

Of all her collector friends, Miss Hogg became closest to Katharine Prentis Murphy. Miss Hogg turned to her, as well as John Graham and John Staub in 1959 as she embarked on her initial interior alterations at Bayou Bend. Ultimately these renovations established settings and interpretative themes that would complement and define her collection. The majority of these changes were planned for the east wing, in spaces originally intended as Will and Mike's "bachelor quarters." Initially, her focus was on a first floor complex, combining a hall, small kitchen, tap room, and bath into one large space that would exhibit the earliest furniture in the collection, the Late Renaissance and Early Baroque periods. Complementing them would be collections of blue and white delftwares and a selection of British and American pewter.

Katharine Prentis Murphy favored these early styles and had previously interpreted them in a series of rooms she assembled for the New Hampshire and New York historical societies. At Bayou Bend, the interior that coalesced, with its paneled wall, distinctive checkerboard floor, and even down to the arrangement of the furniture, bore uncanny similarities to a parlor she created for the New Hampshire Historical Society a year earlier. The Bayou Bend room mirrored Mrs. Murphy's taste and arrangement more so than Miss Hogg's, and Miss Hogg honored her dear friend by naming it for her.[31]

With the Murphy Room completed, Miss Hogg took a different approach for the renovations to the second-floor spaces that became the Chippendale Bedroom, Federal Parlor, and Newport and Texas rooms. She invited a number of her friends to serve as "Honorary Advisors to the Bayou Bend Collection." In addition to Katharine Prentis Murphy and John Graham, the group comprised Ralph Carpenter, Henry Francis du Pont, Henry and Helen Flynt, Maxim Karolik, Donald Shelley, Electra Havemeyer Webb, Alice Winchester and Charles Montgomery. Miss Hogg sent each a questionnaire categorizing the issues she needed to address, an inventory of objects she proposed for these spaces, and inquiries about additional pieces that should be considered to complete them.[32]

Of this group, Charles Montgomery projected the greatest influence and became a mainstay as he helped her maneuver the intricacies of the renovations. He dedicated much time to responding to her questions with the latest scholarship on floor coverings, lighting, and accessories. With the paneled interior for the Newport Room completed, Charles and Florence Montgomery visited Miss Hogg at Bayou Bend. In recounting their colloquium to S. I. Morris, the museum's president, she professed, "My great regret is that the officials of the Houston museum and the members of the Bayou Bend Advisory Committee could not sit in to benefit by the great privilege that was mine to receive the views and recommendations made by Mr. and Mrs. Montgomery. I never dreamed their approach would offer the scope it did."[33]

As Miss Hogg was focused on the room installations at Bayou Bend during the late 1950s and early 1960s, she continued to seek out masterworks. In 1959, a Philadelphia slab table was acquired for the central hall (cat. 30). The following year, Charles Willson Peale's striking *Self-Portrait with Angelica and Portrait of Rachel* came on the market (cat. 43). It was flown down from New York for Miss Hogg to consider, and after a sleepless night she realized that, in spite of its considerable price, she would always regret it if she let it go. Later that year, an easy chair with its brilliant original needlework covers, a remarkable discovery, was acquired (cat. 39). In 1961, three of the sublime Neoclassical side chairs made for the great Salem merchant Elias Hasket Derby became available from his descendants and Miss Hogg purchased a pair (cat. 59); the remaining example was acquired by the Metropolitan Museum of Art.

Miss Hogg began to identify and address a myriad of needs for when Bayou Bend would become a public institution. She recognized that plans could not progress without the support of her neighbors. Space for parking would have to be allocated near a public approach to the property. She determined that a board or committee

should be appointed to oversee the museum, and that the museum would depend on a corps of volunteers to assist in carrying out its programs. A partnership was formed with the River Oaks Garden Club in 1961 to ensure the preservation and maintenance of the fourteen-acre gardens and grounds.[34] About the same time, Miss Hogg began to collaborate with Ruth Pershing Uhler, the director of education at the Museum of Fine Arts, to establish a docent organization. She invited her good friend Eugenia Tennant to chair the group, and subsequently enticed Jonathan Fairbanks, a young protégé of Charles Montgomery's, to train the first class (see fig. 1). The docents were completely devoted to Miss Hogg, and on the occasion of Bayou Bend's public dedication, in March 1966, they honored her by contributing funds for an acquisition.[35] In the intervening years, the docents have continued to support accessions as an organization (cat. 77), through their provisional classes, and individually, including Gloria Garic Anderson (cat. 41), Evelyn Houstoun Chew (cat. 76), Jeanne Cunningham (cat. 93), Ruth Kerridge (cat. 42), and Karen Marrow (cat. 61).

The concept of hiring a full-time curator was broached with Miss Hogg as early as 1955, when Lee Malone wrote, "I believe I mentioned writing to Mr. Montgomery at Winterthur on the subject of a curatorial scholar in the American field. He has given me the very encouraging news that one of the fellows we met in Williamsburg might be available."[36] Malone's correspondence indicates he raised the subject on other occasions, but explains, "hitherto, she has not felt the pressing need of doing so."[37] A decade after having first discussed the idea, Miss Hogg decided it was time to bring a professionally trained curator on board, and in 1965 David B. Warren, a recent graduate of the Winterthur program, was hired (fig. 7). Practically from the very start, the two formed a relationship characterized by compatibility and mutual respect. Within a few weeks of his arrival, Miss Hogg wrote Ed Rotan, the president of the Museum of Fine Arts, Houston, and members of the Bayou Bend

Fig. 6.
The executive committee of the 1998 Theta Charity Antiques Show gathered on the Diana Terrace at Bayou Bend; (back row, left to right:)
Lois Wright, Mary Ruth Benson, Kathy Peveto, Jan Neuenschwander, and Cynthia Adkins; (front row, left to right:) Olivia Munson,
Cheri Fossler, Norma Jean Brown, Carol Sanford, Vicki Lange, and Liz Rigney. Photograph by Gittings.

Advisory Committee: ". . . I could not be more pleased than I am with the selection of David Warren as Curator at Bayou Bend. I think he has great knowledge and intuitive sense which is very valuable, good taste and maturity. I feel that Bayou Bend is going into the right hands and I have always had confidence in those who direct the policies of the Museum of Fine Arts."[38] Although she did not know it at the time, Miss Hogg could have also acknowledged him for his longevity: he remained at Bayou Bend for thirty-eight years, and was named director in 1987. Long after Miss Hogg's death he continues to be a vital link to the founder.

Within a few months of David Warren's arrival, Miss Hogg vacated Bayou Bend for a high-rise apartment, where she would reside for the final decade of her life. Sensitive to the need for him to establish himself at Bayou Bend, a month passed before he heard from her. Then, one afternoon she called. After exchanging pleasantries, she asked him if it would be all right for her to come by for a visit.

Together, the collector and curator resumed the never-ending quest for objects to augment the museum's collection.

1965–75

I am doing exactly what I have always wished to do and I am not reluctant to see Bayou Bend go into hands which I feel confident will appreciate and treasure all that it means. I hope . . . that the future visitor to Bayou Bend will gain a greater reverence for our heritage. . . .

IMA HOGG TO EDWARD ROTAN,
JULY 27, 1965

Bayou Bend was dedicated as a public museum in March 1966. A few months later, the Friends of Bayou Bend was organized. Envisioned as a coalition to benefit programming and operations, the organization's proceeds were also appropriated for collections from 1970 to 1986. During this period, the Friends underwrote a dozen accessions. Foremost among these is a diminutive sauceboat, a great rarity from the earliest American porcelain factory (cat. 44). The group's support also helped fund the acquisition of a splendid likeness of James Cornell Biddle by Thomas Sully (cat. 79).[39]

In large part, the parameters of the Bayou Bend Collection were determined during the 1950s and early 1960s, as Miss Hogg and her coterie of advisors began to orchestrate the room settings throughout the house. As each interior assumed its own distinctive character, interpretive themes and relevant groupings began to emerge. In the decade between 1965 and 1975, accessions were made to refine the collection and address Miss Hogg's priorities. A grand Baroque portrait of Mrs. Samuel McCall by Robert Feke (cat. 15) and John Smibert's companion likenesses of Samuel Pemberton (cat. 12) and his sister, Mary, introduced key works by these seminal artists. Other acquisitions filled out collection areas lacking in depth, such as an exquisite group of silk mourning embroideries (cats. 63 and 65), or the idyllic Texas landscape by the German immigrant Hermann Lungkwitz (cat. 98).

By 1966 the collections at Bayou Bend presented a survey of American art from the seventeenth century through the Federal period. Viewing the history of design as a continuum, Miss Hogg and David Warren then began planning for additional installations to present the subsequent revival styles of the nineteenth century. Within the year they began to work on interiors interpreting the Grecian taste popular in the early part of that century. Acquisitions such as the painted center table manifest the line, scale, and aesthetics of the period—in this instance with a masterfully rendered landscape that coalesces both artist's and cabinetmaker's

Top to bottom:

Fig. 7.
David B. Warren, 2001.
Photograph by Betty Tichich, Houston Chronicle.

Fig. 8.
Betty C. Jukes, founder of the Houston Junior Woman's
Club (second from left), with Bayou Bend docents
(left to right) Patti Mullendore, Toni Wallingford,
and Judy Baldwin, 1999.

sensibilities (cat. 73). In 1969, upon the completion of these interiors, she dedicated and named them for her late friend Dorothy Dawes Chillman, who had studied the French antecedents of this style.

With the Greek Revival stylishly presented by the Chillman Suite, Miss Hogg and David Warren directed their attention towards a completely different aesthetic—the Rococo Revival. As early as 1944, she took a bold and dramatic step when she purchased a seven-piece Rococo Revival parlor suite.[40] Among collectors of her generation, Miss Hogg was unique in her advocacy of this style. For her contemporaries, it may have been all too familiar; an interest in early American decorative arts was for many a personal reaction to the excesses of the nineteenth century that they had grown up with. Her attraction to this furniture may be attributed to her prescience in collecting, but it also may have been prompted by cherished memories of her childhood and family. Years later, she related the impression that old furniture had made on her as a young girl: "I cannot remember when I was not interested in old things with a history. My maternal grandfather, Colonel James Stinson's house in East Texas was filled with ante-bellum furniture, long out of fashion, and at the Governor's Mansion in Austin, I slept in Sam Houston's mahogany four-poster tester bed."[41]

Fortuitously, as Miss Hogg and David Warren planned for the Belter Parlor at Bayou Bend, they learned of the availability of a remarkably complete group of interior fixtures: a Wilton carpet, a heavily carved marble mantle, complete with its gilded overmantle mirror and valances, and a cut-glass gas chandelier, all of which had been assembled in the George Corliss mansion in Providence, Rhode Island. Together with a wallpaper and border reproduced from French originals selected for Elmwood, a house built in Salisbury, Connecticut about 1850, they created a setting for the furniture, paintings, and related decorative arts that would be distinguished as the last and latest of the interiors at Bayou Bend—and its most historically accurate installation.[42]

Although the efficacy of Miss Hogg's collecting on Houstonians has never been fully assessed, it can be inferred from a variety of sources. One of these is the success and longevity of the annual Theta Charity Antiques Show (figs. 6 and 9). In 1952, Houston alumnae of the Kappa Alpha Theta sorority organized an antiques show, which today is distinguished as the most senior of these philanthropic events in the country. Practically from the start, Miss Hogg, in her unobtrusive way, lent her support. When asked, she confided her opinions of the dealers being considered or offered suggestions for forum speakers. She supported the show through her purchases and by entertaining the dealers and the lecturers at Bayou Bend. In 1969, the Thetas recognized Miss Hogg for her substantive contributions by dedicating that year's show in her honor and designating a portion of the proceeds towards an accession for Bayou Bend. Ever since, their support has been unfailing, and with their contributions now in excess of one million dollars, the Thetas are the principal benefactor to Bayou Bend's accessions fund.[43] Many purchases funded by the Thetas have enhanced the collection's strengths, perhaps most notably in portraiture. Works by such major artists as John Hesselius (cat. 14), John Trumbull (cat. 48), and Rembrandt Peale have been introduced. The Thetas' generosity is not only observable in their annual contributions, but can also be perceived in the spirit of their philanthropy, never encumbering their largesse by attaching to it a set of conditions. When the museum approached them with a rare, but diminutive silver dram cup, by John Hull and Robert Sanderson, Sr., they understood its significance and affirmed the decision to purchase it (cat. 4).

Another service organization that has had a tremendous impact on Bayou Bend since the late 1960s is Houston Junior Woman's Club. Established in 1968, the timing of its founding could not have been more fortuitous for Bayou Bend. Although the museum was opened two years earlier, the public's access on weekends was limited since the core of docents was not sufficient to offer weekend tours. Under the leadership of Betty C. Jukes (fig. 8), Houston Junior Woman's Club committed to hosting the monthly Family Day, and has done so ever since. A year later, in 1969, the organization made its first gift to Bayou Bend.[44] Their contributions have been dedicated to accessions, and more recently, to supporting the museum's education programs as well. In keeping with the club's mission, many of these acquisitions have been prominent in furthering the institution's educational role. Notable among these is the Amelung tumbler engraved with the word "Federal," heralding the establishment of the federal government in 1788; it is the most important piece of glass in the collection (cat. 54). Subsequently, Houston Junior Woman's Club lent considerable support in the effort to secure the significant collection of early Texas pottery by the Wilson family (cat. 90).

Since the public dedication of Bayou Bend in 1966, and over the intervening years, Miss Hogg must have taken great satisfaction in the development of the institution—perhaps no more so than in 1975, as collector and curator worked toward the publication of *Bayou Bend: American Furniture, Paintings and Silver from the Bayou Bend Collection*, the first scholarly catalogue on any aspect of the collections of the Museum of Fine Arts, Houston. As David Warren related in his introduction, the volume was intended to make Bayou Bend more widely known and accessible. Warren was assisted in this endeavor by Dean F. Failey, a Winterthur graduate who joined the curatorial staff from 1971 to 1974. Subsequently Barry A. Greenlaw and Katherine S. Howe collaborated with Warren in the latter half of the 1970s, and in 1980, Michael K. Brown joined the staff.

Ima Hogg stands apart from other decorative arts collectors not only of her own generation but of subsequent generations as well. When in her nineties, having filled practically every available space at Bayou Bend, she contemplated further extending the collection's parameters

to the late nineteenth and early twentieth centuries. In 1975, she articulated her intent to acquire one of Louis Comfort Tiffany's iconic lamps, or examples of the Arts and Crafts pottery produced at Newcomb College (cat. 100).[45] She had hardly begun on this latest foray when she died, unexpectedly, that September while traveling abroad. Miss Hogg's vision of the Bayou Bend Collection was as an eloquent compendium of American art—one that, had she had not run out of space and time, would have spanned from the early seventeenth century through the beginning of the twentieth. Within a year of her death, the Museum of Fine Arts affirmed this vision, and established a department of decorative arts, under the aegis of Katherine Howe, that would collect the later periods Miss Hogg was beginning to explore.

In 1976, a compelling likeness of Dr. Mason Fitch Cogswell by Ralph Earl, an artist Miss Hogg had long sought for the collection, was acquired in her memory (cat. 52). It could not have been a more fitting tribute to this remarkable woman. The acquisition of the Earl portrait, while honoring Miss Hogg, also reflected her intent that the museum's collection, with the support of others, would continue to evolve.

1975–2007

One aspect of Ima Hogg's legacy was her ability to teach by example. Since her death the trustees and supporters of the museum have continued her tradition of collecting and improving Bayou Bend. . . .

PETER C. MARZIO, 1989

Miss Ima Hogg generously gave Bayou Bend a magnificent collection, as well as a handsome endowment to help support the museum's operations. It was her intent and belief that others

Top to bottom:

Fig. 9.
Representatives of the Theta Charity Antiques Show at the 50th anniversary show in 2002; (left to right:) Mary Frances Couper, chairman of the second show; Martha Taylor Jones, chairman of the 50th anniversary show; and Mary Margaret McDonald, chairman of the first show.

Fig. 10.
Mr. and Mrs. W. H. Keenan.

Top to bottom:

Fig. 11.
Mr. and Mrs. William S. Kilroy, 1993.
Photograph by Temple Webber Photography.

Fig. 12.
Jack McGregor (left) with artist Salvador Dali
in the 1960s. Photograph by Paul Cordes;
The Museum of Fine Arts, Houston, Archives.

would share in the development of Bayou Bend, whether it be furthering the museum's educational mission, helping to preserve its landscaped gardens, or contributing towards operating expenses and maintenance. Miss Hogg did not designate monies for an accessions fund, but she provided for acquisitions in a different manner—through the friendships and relationships she had cultivated over the years. The concept of establishing an oversight committee for Bayou Bend was considered as early as February 1957, some months prior to Miss Hogg's giving the property to the Museum of Fine Arts.[46] While the ideas discussed at the time were never acted on, by February 1960 the Bayou Bend Committee was established.[47] Over the years, a number of Miss Hogg's friends would be asked to serve on the board. Many were collectors themselves, including James L. Britton, Jr. (fig. 15, cats. 26, 27, and 29), Mary Frances Couper (fig. 9, cat. 34), Mr. and Mrs. Robert D. Jameson (cat. 58), W. H. Keenan (fig. 10, cats. 55 and 87), Mr. and Mrs. William S. Kilroy, Sr. (fig. 11, cat. 8) and Harris Masterson III (fig. 4, cat. 23). These individuals, who came to support the institution in a variety of ways, made gifts from their own collections, or generously underwrote acquisitions.

In her later years, Miss Hogg drafted lists of objects she sought for the collection. In 1952, as she began to ask Vincent Andrus for assistance, she compiled just such a list for him.[48] These drafts proved meaningful as she planned for Bayou Bend's future. A year before her death, in 1974, she worked with David Warren to update the document.[49] For both the committee members and staff, this instrument has provided an ongoing guide for acquisitions. A number of the objects enumerated on it have been added to the collection, including the "Wainscot Chair" (cat. 1), "Tall Clock" (cat. 11), "Stand or Guéridon" (cat. 87), "an example by Hull and Sanderson" (cat. 4), "examples from the Amelung Factory" (cat. 54), and "an example by Jonathan Trumbull" (cat. 48).

The priority list is invaluable as a guide,

though the trustees and staff recognize its limitations. Simply because an object is not specified does not imply that it would not make a meaningful addition to the collection. In 1979, just such a circumstance presented itself when the acquisition of a Pennsylvania German painted cupboard was discussed. Years earlier, Miss Hogg observed that a painted cupboard used to display historical blue Staffordshire should be upgraded when a finer example became available.[50] By happenstance, at the Theta Charity Antiques Show, a superb example in a remarkable state of preservation was offered (cat. 50). Although not recorded on the priority list, it represented a major potential acquisition for the museum. Weighing the significance of the piece, and recognizing that it would have to be installed with Pennsylvania redware because it would be incongruous if it were filled with the historical Staffordshire, the committee agreed and endorsed the change. Staffordshire Hall was no more; the space was reinstalled and renamed Pennsylvania-German Hall. This acquisition, made only a few years after Miss Hogg's death, signifies that the committee members and staff were mindful of her dictum that the Bayou Bend Collection should thoughtfully evolve.

Within two years, another interior, the Belter Parlor, underwent a major reinstallation. Shortly after the room was completed in 1971, Miss Hogg purchased the only documented, intact suite of furniture from John Henry Belter's shop (cat. 91).[51] With the room's carefully coordinated reproduction upholstery and drapery having been completed only two years earlier, Miss Hogg was reluctant to completely redo the interior, and instead she decided to give the newly acquired furniture to the Texas Governor's Mansion. By 1981, the Governor's Mansion was undergoing a major renovation. Members of the refurbishing committee evaluated the importance of the Belter suite against the day-to-day use it sustained in the mansion and decided that the set should revert to Bayou Bend, in accordance with Miss Hogg's deed of gift. As with the Pennsylvania cupboard two years earlier, the acquisition reaffirmed a policy that change was permitted if it would enhance the collection.

The Belter suite raised another issue, which was how large a collection the museum should sustain. In turn, this question prompted a discussion on deaccessioning. The furniture under debate was a Rococo Revival sofa and pair of side chairs that Miss Hogg had acquired earlier; although not documented, they were virtually identical to the other set.[52] Committee members and staff recognized that each acquisition is accompanied by a commitment of time and expense to record, research, store, and conserve it. The decision was made to deaccession the three pieces, send them to auction and the funds realized would be designated for acquisitions, in accord with the policies of the Museum of Fine Arts, Houston.

The proceeds from the sale of the Rococo Revival seating furniture were ultimately combined with a generous gift from William J. Hill (fig. 16) to underwrite the acquisition of a major piece of early southern silver, a high priority for the collection. The classically inspired vase by Charleston silversmith John Ewan, the most significant work by a nineteenth-century Charleston silversmith, had been presented to the Reverend Samuel Gilman in 1832 (cat. 75). Another important southern urban center, Baltimore, has also been more fully represented in the collection. In 1980, the imposing soup tureen by Andrew Ellicott Warner, from a dinner service the citizens of Baltimore presented to Commodore Stephen Decatur, was underwritten by the Thetas (cat. 71). Subsequently, a monumental example by Warner's chief competitor, Samuel Kirk, was introduced in the form of an exuberantly executed Rococo-inspired water pitcher (cat. 95).

The decorative arts of the American South had long interested Miss Hogg; however, at the time she was collecting, they were not widely known or recognized, as confirmed by a letter from Charles Montgomery: "Charleston furniture is going to be slow to come, but I think you will get some with patience."[53] Southern silver,

as well as painting and other decorative arts, remain a priority, and in recent years some major examples, such as the early South Carolina great chair (cat. 5) and the superlative pair of satinwood card tables (cat. 55), have been added.

The annual event "One Great Night in November" has been a force in the development of the Bayou Bend Collection. As Peter C. Marzio, director of the Museum of Fine Arts, Houston, has related, in 1983 William J. Hill proposed the idea that the museum should host an old-time, black-tie smoker to raise funds for the museum's collections.[54] Many attending the annual event over the years have displayed a penchant for American art, underwriting more than one hundred accessions for Bayou Bend. While representing almost every medium, approximately one third of these are American prints, including Amos Doolittle's celebrated *A Display of the United States of America*, John Bower's depiction of the bombardment of Fort McHenry in the War of 1812, and L. H. Bradford & Co.'s serene view of Gloucester Harbor after Fitz Henry Lane (cats. 57, 72, and 92). It is unclear why Miss Hogg never assembled a more comprehensive survey of prints. In recent times a greater emphasis has been placed on developing the museum's print collection. Engraved images were long a popular fixture in the American home. The extensive range of subject matter offers an unparalleled perspective on American culture.

Miss Hogg also did not collect textiles in any depth. Her most notable purchases were acquired as part of upholstered furniture: the card table that descended in the Faneuil family, and the easy chair with its magnificent Irish stitch, or flamestitch, cover (cats. 13 and 39). According to David Warren, she recognized the challenges of maintaining and storing antique textiles in Houston's hot, humid climate and for that reason the museum's textile collection today remains modest. A few select additions have expanded the representation, including a charming naive sampler worked by Polly Snow and dated 1798, the gift of Mr. and Mrs. James

Top to bottom:

Fig. 13.
Mrs. James Anderson, Jr., 1999.
Photograph by Michael Carr Photography.

Fig. 14.
The Brown Foundation, Inc., is represented on the Bayou Bend Committee by Isabel B. Wilson, who also serves as chairman of the Board of Trustees of the Museum of Fine Arts, Houston, and Nancy O'Connor Abendshein, 2006. Photograph by Rick Gardner.

Top to bottom:

Fig. 15
Mr. and Mrs. James L. Britton, Jr., 1982.

Fig. 16
William J. Hill, 1990.

Marrow (cat. 61), and an embroidered coat of arms, which is particularly significant for its documentation: "Wrought by H[ann]ah Babcock at Mrs. Snow's school, Pemberton Hills, Boston, 1785 (cat. 64)." This old, yellowed label contributed toward a reinterpretation of these objects as examples of schoolgirl embroidery.

As the Bayou Bend Collection has evolved, it has proven beneficial to periodically review and assess the museum's holdings. In 1985, a team of conservators was engaged to evaluate the museum's exhibition practices and maintenance requirements, as well as to assess the condition of the collection. The project was awarded funding by each of the agencies approached— the Getty Grant Program of the J. Paul Getty Trust, the Institute of Museum Services, the National Endowment for the Arts, the Cultural Arts Council of Houston, and the Texas State Historical Commission.[55] The central conclusion derived from this process was the museum's need for a staff conservator to oversee the collection's care, to undertake special treatments, and to advise on accessions and deaccessions. In 1990, Steven L. Pine was hired, the first full-time conservator on the staff of the Museum of Fine Arts, Houston.

Coinciding with the conservation survey was a related survey of the collection that would bolster plans for an updated collection catalogue.[56] Whereas the 1975 edition comprised furniture, painting, and silver, this proposed volume would include all of the media, and record them in more extensive detail than had previously been done. Together, these dual surveys had a significant impact in terms of more fully understanding the collection. These substantive endeavors ultimately led to a more critical assessment of the works. The comprehensive, scholarly catalogue *American Decorative Arts and Paintings in the Bayou Bend Collection* was published in 1998 by the Museum of Fine Arts, Houston, and Princeton University Press. It was made possible by the support of the Henry R. Luce Foundation and the National Endowment for the Arts.

Almost from the very start, Miss Hogg under-

stood that the collection would have to be fluid if it were to improve and expand. In 1949, when giving the museum three pieces of furniture, she wrote James Chillman: "You have already seen and approved these pieces, as have various other experts, and I feel reasonably sure that the museum will make no mistake accepting them for a permanent collection. However, I wish to say that if ever it is desired that any one of these pieces could be exchanged for a better one of the same type and period, I would readily consent as I feel sure the museum would."[57] This philosophy would continue to be incorporated in Miss Hogg's proffers of gifts. She could see little justification for duplicates and, aside from the need to allow light-sensitive objects such as textiles and works on paper to rest during part of the year, she did not believe in relegating major portions of the collection to storage.

Beginning in 1990, the museum staff undertook a rigorous review of the collection, as well as a large number of objects that the executors of Miss Hogg's estate had designated for Bayou Bend but were not appropriate for the collection. Some of these pieces were retained by the museum's education department, but the majority were offered at public sale. In April 1992, Hart Galleries in Houston published a catalogue and auctioned 675 lots from Bayou Bend.[58] Once commissions and expenses were deducted, the net proceeds were earmarked for accessions, in accordance with museum policy.

As Bayou Bend's collection priorities are so specific, six years would pass before the proceeds from the Hart sale were depleted. For the most part they were dedicated to the purchase of two seventeenth-century great chairs, pieces that elevated the museum's small aggregate of early furniture. Although contemporary in date, they are disparate in terms of their origin and production. The first, referred to as a wainscot chair because of its distinctive mortise-and-tenon construction, had long been a priority of Miss Hogg's (cat. 1). This Essex County, Massachusetts, example was acquired in 1875 by James Little of Brookline, Massachusetts, and was sold by his descendants. By comparison, the other chair was the work of a turner, as compared to a joiner who constructed the New England chair. A relatively recent discovery, scholars herald it as the earliest identified example of South Carolina furniture (cat. 5).

The Museum of Fine Arts, Houston, established several curatorial departments in the 1990s toward furthering its mission as an encyclopedic institution embracing all cultures and periods. In 1991, a department of prints and drawings was established with Barry Walker as curator, and a department of textiles and costume was founded under the aegis of Elizabeth Ann Coleman. Both curators generously lent their expertise to Bayou Bend for issues regarding collection care and acquisitions. In 1995, the Department of American Painting and Sculpture was formed with Emily Ballew Neff as its curator. Dr. Neff had been awarded the Jameson Fellowship in 1989–90, while a graduate student at Rice University, which provided her with the opportunity to work intimately with the collection. Under her curatorial guidance, a number of thoughtful additions have been made to the collection.

Miss Hogg assembled a notable survey of American portraiture, spanning from the beginning of the eighteenth century through the middle of the nineteenth. Since 1975, works by artists central to the history of American painting have been added to the collection, including John Trumbull (cat. 48), Raphaelle Peale, and Thomas Sully (cat. 79). Other additions contributed toward broadening the collection's range. The admirable body of work by Charles Willson Peale was augmented by an example demonstrating the artist's proficiency in miniature (cat. 42), a gift of Mr. and Mrs. Isaac C. Kerridge. A picturesque Peale landscape was a gift of Nancy Glanville Jewell, a dedicated member of the Bayou Bend Committee (cat. 67). The beginning of the American still-life tradition is represented by James Peale's lush painting of vegetables (cat. 68), funded by the Thetas. William J. Hill's gift of Erastus Dow Palmer's *Infant Flora* (cat. 86) introduced academic sculpture to the collection.

Early in her collecting, Miss Hogg recognized the significance of John Hesselius as the principal artist working in the Philadelphia area during the third quarter of the eighteenth century. Scholars had long puzzled over the authorship of the group portrait she had acquired in 1960. In the 1980s it was convincingly reassigned to a contemporary British painter, Arthur Devis. In 2003, Hesselius was once again restored to the pantheon of American artists at Bayou Bend with the acquisition of an ambitious double portrait depicting Mrs. Matthew Tilghman and her young daughter, Anna Maria (cat. 14). A major addition to the museum's collection, the painting was given jointly by the Thetas and The Brown Foundation, Inc. (fig. 14) to honor David B. Warren on his retirement.

Bayou Bend's first endowed accessions fund was established by Mrs. W. H. Keenan in 1998. Billy and Marion Keenan (fig. 10) were great enthusiasts of American history and art, and Mr. Keenan was a member of the Bayou Bend Committee. Following the death of her husband, Mrs. Keenan began to consider how she might honor him through a gift to Bayou Bend. She came to recognize the long-term benefit of an endowment and chose to establish the W. H. Keenan Family Endowment Fund. Since then, the Keenan family has continued to augment the fund. Today, the fund is the oldest and the largest of Bayou Bend's accessions endowments.

The establishment of the W. H. Keenan Family Endowment Fund prompted the Bayou Bend Docent Organization, chaired by Susie Glasscock, to establish a comparable fund, also in 1998. Within the next three years, two more endowments were created. In 1999, with the encouragement of Ralph O'Connor, the Marian and Speros Martel Foundation established a fund in honor of William S. Kilroy Sr. Avid collectors of American art and Bayou Bend supporters, Bill and Jeanie Kilroy (fig. 11) have both been members of the Bayou Bend Committee. A fourth fund was created in 2001 from a bequest made by Jack R. McGregor (fig. 12), who was formerly a

museum professional and later an antiques dealer. When he died in 2000, he left the bulk of his estate to the museum, requesting that the monies be applied towards the acquisition of glass (cat. 78). In 2006 and 2007, Mrs. Kilroy, Dr. and Mrs. David Ott, Mrs. James Anderson, Jr. (fig. 13), Houston Junior Woman's Club, and Toni and Ralph Wallingford designated funds for Bayou Bend accessions endowments.

Although the majority of the museum's acquisitions are underwritten through financial donations, the most significant direct gift of objects came to Bayou Bend through a 1999 bequest from Mr. and Mrs. James L. Britton, Jr. (fig. 15, cats. 26, 27, and 29). Great friends of Miss Hogg, they shared her passion for Americana, as well as for Texana. Marian Britton served as a trustee of the Museum of Fine Arts, and her husband and both sons were members of the Bayou Bend Committee. The Brittons were enamored with the superb design and craftsmanship of furniture produced in Newport, Rhode Island, and their magnificent gift transformed the Newport Room at Bayou Bend.

While the Bayou Bend Collection was envisioned as an assemblage of American art that would reflect the Anglo culture that founded the United States, Miss Hogg was equally fascinated by her native state's history, and she conveyed her pride through an interior that paid homage to Texas. Completed in 1961, the Texas Room installation underscored the limited scholarship available, which held that there were few craftsmen working in Texas as most settlers simply brought their furniture and other possessions with them. Just a few years later, this interpretation was dismissed, as more was learned about artists and artisans who worked in Texas. Not surprisingly, Miss Hogg was in part responsible for encouraging this increased scholarship.[59] Today, the Texana at Bayou Bend more fully reflects these scholarly advances: since 1975, examples of Texas furniture, silver, pottery, textiles, and paintings have been added to more fully represent the rich material culture of the Lone Star State. In 1982, with the acquisition of a unique stoneware jar from Jefferson S. Nash's Marion County pottery, the museum began to explore this area; its holdings were completely transformed in 2001 with the purchase of a small, but choice, group of early Texas pottery. Predominant was the work of the African-American artisans employed at John Wilson's and Hyrum Wilson's potteries outside Seguin (cat. 90). The latter, established about 1869, is believed to be the earliest business organized, owned, and operated by African Americans in Texas. With support from thirteen donors, the collection was secured for Bayou Bend and, in doing so, the museum found itself with one of the most significant collections of Texas African-American pottery in any public institution.[60] The arts of Texas at Bayou Bend were greatly augmented in 2005 through a sequence of important gifts and loans from William J. Hill (cat. 99). The furniture that Miss Hogg had assembled for the Texas Room, reflecting what the early settlers could have brought with them to Texas, was replaced by an installation of thirteen pieces attributed to Johann Michael Jahn and the other skilled German cabinetmakers who settled the Texas Hill Country.

Important works that illustrate the chapters of our American past continue to benefit the collection. Under the leadership of Bonnie A. Campbell, who was appointed director of Bayou Bend in 2004, and Peter C. Marzio, director of the Museum of Fine Arts, Houston, the museum has reaffirmed its view of Bayou Bend as a dynamic entity. As Miss Hogg stated in her foreword to Bayou Bend: American Furniture, Paintings and Silver from the Bayou Bend Collection, "The Bayou Bend Collection was always designed for the public."[61] Most certainly, she intended her comment to refer to the museum visitor, but in keeping with the progressive philosophy that was central to her outlook, she no doubt also envisioned the collection as one in which the public would participate—as trustees, volunteers, and donors. Her belief is reaffirmed by this handsome volume, which illustrates and describes fifty major acquisitions that are the gifts of other donors in addition to fifty given by Miss Hogg. In all, of the 5,200 objects that presently comprise the Bayou Bend Collection, approximately 1,700 are gifts from more than 400 donors. Engaged with the museum staff, these individuals, organizations, foundations, and corporations share Ima Hogg's vision and continue to build on the foundation that she created.

1. Ima Hogg, foreword to *Bayou Bend: American Furniture, Paintings and Silver from the Bayou Bend Collection* by David B. Warren (Houston: The Museum of Fine Arts, Houston; Boston: New York Graphic Society, 1975): vii–viii. At this time, Ima Hogg was suffering from a succession of illnesses that persisted through 1924; see Kate Sayen Kirkland, "Envisioning a Progressive City: Hogg Family Philanthropy and the Urban Ideal in Houston, Texas, 1910–1975" (Ph.D. diss., Rice University, 2004): 71–74. In September 1920, Will Hogg embarked on his own collecting odyssey and began to form an extensive assemblage of the work of Frederic Remington. In 1943, his sister gave these works to the Museum of Fine Arts, Houston; see Emily Ballew Neff, *Frederic Remington: The Hogg Brothers Collection of the Museum of Fine Arts, Houston* (Princeton: Princeton University Press, 2000).

2. For a more detailed history and analysis of the Hogg family's philanthropy, see Neff, *Frederic Remington*, 7–16, and Kirkland, *Hogg Family Philanthropy*. The definitive biography on Governor Hogg remains Robert C. Cotner, *James Stephen Hogg: A Biography* (Austin: University of Texas Press, 1959).

3. The most comprehensive study that chronicles the history of collecting American antiques is Elizabeth Stillinger's *The Antiquers: The Lives and Careers, the Deals, the Finds, the Collections of the Men and Women Who Were Responsible for the Changing Taste in American Antiques, 1850–1930* (New York: Alfred A. Knopf, 1980). See also Charles B. Hosmer, Jr., *Presence of the Past: A History of the Preservation Movement in the United States before Williamsburg* (New York: G. P. Putnam's Sons, 1965).

4. For the history of the Pendleton Collection, see Christopher P. Monkhouse and Thomas S. Michie, *American Furniture in Pendleton House* (Providence: Museum of Art, Rhode Island School of Design, 1986). For the Hudson-Fulton Exhibition, see Calvin Tomkins, *Merchants and Masterpieces: The Story of the Metropolitan Museum of Art* (New York: Henry Holt, 1989), 195–98, and Stillinger, *The Antiquers*, 128–31.

5. Wendell Garrett and Allison Eckardt Ledes, "Seventy-Five Years of *The Magazine Antiques*, 1922–1997," *Antiques* 151, no. 1 (January 1997): 178–183.

6. In addition, the library included titles on ceramics by John Spargo and N. Hudson Moore; glass by Rhea Mansfield Knittle, Mary Harrod Northend, Lenore Wheeler Williams, and Stephen Van Rensselaer; silver by Francis Hill Bigelow and Arthur Hayden; ironwork by J. S. Gardner; oriental rugs by G. G. Lewis; as well as complementary volumes on early American painting and architecture. "Miss Ima Hogg Inventory and Appraisement of Furniture and Furnishings at Bayou Bend, Houston, Texas, as of June 25, 1933," 50, 53, 54, 59, 60, the Museum of Fine Arts, Houston, Archives (MFAH Archives).

7. Will Hogg to Ima Hogg, 28 February 1921. William Clifford Hogg Papers, Center for American History, The University of Texas at Austin.

8. Neff, *Frederic Remington*, 10, 12, 16–19, 22–26. As Neff points out, the penthouse interiors were pictured and published in Dorothy M. Hoskins, "American Furniture of Early Date," *Civics for Houston* 1, no. 6 (June 1928): 6–7.

9. Morrison H. Heckscher, *The Metropolitan Museum of Art: An Architectural History*," The Metropolitan Museum of Art Bulletin (Summer 1995): 54–55; A copy of R. T. H. Halsey and Charles O. Cornelius's *A Handbook of the American Wing Opening Exhibition* (New York: The Metropolitan Museum of Art, 1924) appears in the "Miss Ima Hogg Inventory," 1933, MFAH Archives.

10. Although Birdsall Briscoe and Staub were retained as the architects of record, the design and finished house are credited solely to Staub. Howard Barnstone, *The Architecture of John F. Staub: Houston and the South* (Austin: University of Texas Press, 1979), 106–113. Cornelius wrote an article on Staub's own residence: Charles O. Cornelius, "Transplanting the Eastern Tradition: The Residence of Mrs. John F. Staub, in Houston, Texas of Which John F. Staub was the Architect," *The House Beautiful* 62 (January 1928): 28. Cheryl Caldwell Ferguson, "River Oaks: 1920s Suburban Planning and Development in Houston," *Southwestern Historical Quarterly* (Texas State Historical Association) 104, no. 2 (October 2000). See also Neff, *Frederic Remington*) 19–22, and David B. Warren, *Bayou Bend Gardens: A Southern Oasis* (Houston: The Museum of Fine Arts, Houston; London: Scala Publishers, 2006), 12–15.

11. Barnstone, *John F. Staub*, 106–113; Warren, *Bayou Bend Gardens*, 15–22.

12. "Miss Ima Hogg Inventory," p. 8, MFAH Archives. The most detailed recounting of this exhibition can be found in Wendy Cooper, *In Praise of America: American Decorative Arts, 1650–1830, Fifty Years of Discovery Since the 1929 Girl Scouts Loan Exhibition* (New York: Alfred A. Knopf, 1980), 4–13.

13. For a more extensive treatment of Miss Hogg's works on paper, see Naomi Kroll, "Ima Hogg's Twentieth-Century Collection," Bayou Bend Docent Organization records, MFAH Archives, and Kirkland, "Hogg Family Philanthropy," 414–417. In 1939, Miss Hogg gave the Museum of Fine Arts her collection of more than one hundred works on paper by late nineteenth- and early twentieth-century masters.

14. See Warren, *Bayou Bend Gardens*, for a detailed account of these activities.

15. Among the generous provisions enumerated by Will Hogg's estate was a bequest that was used to establish a foundation. He challenged his siblings to match this legacy, specifying that whoever did so would define the foundation's mission. Ima took up the charge and established the Hogg Foundation for Mental Health in 1939 with an endowment of $2.25 million.

16. Kirkland, "Hogg Family Philanthropy," 469–470.

17. Will of Mike Hogg, no. 31,414, County Clerk's Office, Harris County, Texas, filed on November 17, 1941. Elizabeth Morford, "History in Houses: The Varner-Hogg Plantation in Texas," *Antiques* 76, no. 2 (August 1959): 126–129.

18. Letter from Ima Hogg to S. I. Morris, 16 August 1960, Ima Hogg Papers, Bayou Bend: correspondence, MFAH Archives. When the first class of docents met in 1961, she reiterated Dudley's suggestion to them, and again in her remarks at the public dedication in 1966.

19. By contrast to the other collections Miss Hogg formed, there is little documentation about her Southwest Indian art. For a brief account, see Kirkland, "Hogg Family Philanthropy," 417–420.

20. The most extensive sources on the history of the symphony are Hubert Roussel, *The Houston Symphony Orchestra, 1913–1971* (Austin: University of Texas Press, 1972); Kirkland, "Hogg Family Philanthropy," 359–369.

21. Ima Hogg to Joseph Downs, 18 October 1946, series 2: curatorial/American Wing, correspondence: Joseph Downs, Metropolitan Museum of Art Archives.

22. Correspondence between Ima Hogg and Joseph Downs, 18 October 1946–20 September 1948; between James Chillman and Downs, 10 September 1946–20 September 1948, Series 2: curatorial/American Wing, correspondence: Joseph Downs, Metropolitan Museum of Art Archives. Chillman to Downs, 10 September 1946; Joseph Downs to James Chillman, 31 August 1948; Chillman to Downs, 10 September 1946, director's records, James H. Chillman, Jr., correspondence, RG 2:1, series 2, box 1, MFAH Archives.

23. Correspondence between Vincent Andrus and Ima Hogg, James Chillman, Jr., and Lee Malone, 6 April 1950–3 January 1958, Series 2: curatorial/American Wing, correspondence: Vincent Andrus, Metropolitan Museum of Art Archives. Andrus to Ima Hogg, 13 February 1953; Malone to Andrus, 24 June 1953; Malone to Andrus, 7 July 1953; Ima Hogg to Andrus, July 8, 1953; Andrus to Ima Hogg, 14 January 1955; Ima Hogg to Andrus, 10 February 1956; Andrus to Ima Hogg, 15 February 1956, Bayou Bend dealer/collector files, RG17, series 8, box 7, MFAH Archives.

24. Vincent Andrus to Ima Hogg, 10 July 1953, Series 2: curatorial/ American Wing, correspondence: Vincent Andrus, Metropolitan Museum of Art Archives. "As to the method of your acquisition of silver, I don't think I should buy for you, since I am buying for the Metropolitan and in a small way for myself. I am being perfectly candid because I know there would be times when I would feel like acquiring something that would be suitable for your collection and for the Met. I hope you understand this point and of course if anything is offered to you first I will give you my honest opinion and just make an attempt to get it for the Met or myself."

25. Ima Hogg to Lee Malone, November 3, 1953, Bayou Bend correspondence, MFAH Archives.

26. Stephen Fox, "The Museum of Fine Arts, Houston: An Architectural History, 1924–1986," *The Museum of Fine Arts, Houston, Bulletin*, n. s. 15, special bulletin (1992); Letter from Lee Malone to Ima Hogg, 21 June 1956, Bayou Bend, Misc. Subjects, 1950s–1966, MFAH Archives. Malone's missive makes clear that the museum would not have sufficient exhibition space to accommodate Miss Hogg's collection: "I only wish that we had adequate space to exhibit the many and extremely fine gifts that you have given us over the years but, as you know, this will not be possible pending an expansion of our building plans for the future."

27. Ima Hogg, "Katharine Prentis Murphy," 1968, p. 1, Ima Hogg Papers, Center for American History, The University of Texas at Austin.

28. Ima Hogg to Vincent Andrus, January 27, 1953, Series 2: curatorial/American Wing, correspondence: Vincent Andrus, Metropolitan Museum of Art Archives.

29. I am indebted to Donna Cooke of the Colonial Williamsburg Foundation, who surveyed the Antiques Forum rosters on my behalf. Miss Hogg first attended in 1953, participating in the first session. The following years, 1954 and 1955, she returned, this time for the second session. In 1960, she came for the second session and again in 1962, when Jonathan Fairbanks presented a lecture, "The Bayou Bend Collection at Houston, Texas." She registered for the 1972 forum, "The Arts in the South," where David Warren was presenting a lecture, "Southern Silver," in the second session; however, not feeling well, she cancelled her plans. Copies of the programs and rosters can be found in Historic Restorations: Antiques Forum, ephemera, Ima Hogg Papers, Bayou Bend: renovations, RG MS21, series 1 and 2, box 5, MFAH Archives.

30. Maxim Karolik to Ima Hogg, n.d., Ima Hogg Papers, Bayou Bend correspondence, MFAH Archives.

31. Katharine Prentis Murphy's life and collecting are discussed in Stillinger, *The Antiquers*, 248–251. Upon Mrs. Murphy's death, Miss Hogg composed a written tribute. Ima Hogg Papers, Center for American History, The University of Texas at Austin. Alice Winchester, "Period Rooms for New Hampshire," *Antiques* 74, no. 6 (December 1958), 532–533.

32. List, 14 September 1960, Bayou Bend, misc. subjects, MFAH Archives. Included among Miss Hogg's papers is a four-page response to a letter she sent to Mrs. George Maurice Morris, who had so carefully restored the Lindens in Washington, D.C. Miss Hogg solicited Mrs. Morris's advice in planning her changes at Bayou Bend; Miriam H. Morris to Ima Hogg, 20 November 1956, Ima Hogg Papers, Bayou Bend correspondence, MFAH Archives.

33. Ima Hogg to S. I. Morris, 16 August 1960, MFAH Archives. Montgomery had begun his career as an antiques dealer and early on developed an expertise on American pewter. Perhaps his most visible influence on Miss Hogg's collecting is evident in this medium. In 1960, he sent her a copy of Carl Jacobs's *Guide to American Pewter*, which he annotated for her, noting certain makers he believed should be represented in her collection. Miss Hogg's copy is housed in the Bayou Bend library. Carl Jacobs, *Guide to American Pewter* (New York: The McBride Company, Inc., 1957).

34. The history of this partnership between the River Oaks Garden Club and the Museum of Fine Arts is detailed in Warren, *Bayou Bend Gardens*, 56–63.

35. Bayou Bend Advisory Committee minutes, 15 April 1966, MFAH Archives.

36. Lee Malone to Ima Hogg, 4 April 1955, Bayou Bend correspondence, MFAH Archives.

37. Lee Malone to F. G. Coates, 4 February 1957, Bayou Bend misc. subjects, MFAH Archives.

38. Ima Hogg to Ed Rotan and the Bayou Bend Advisory Committee, 12 August 1965, MFAH Archives.

39. Bayou Bend Advisory Committee minutes, 12 October 1965; 1 November 1967, MFAH Archives.

40. See David B. Warren, et al., *American Decorative Arts and Paintings in the Bayou Bend Collection* (Houston: The Museum of Fine Arts, Houston; Princeton: Princeton University Press, 1998), 144, cat. F233.

41. Warren, *Bayou Bend*, vii.

42. David B. Warren, "Recent Acquisitions, The Belter Parlor at Bayou Bend," *The Museum of Fine Arts, Houston, Bulletin*, n.s. 2, no. 3 (1971): 30–36. The concept for a Rococo Revival parlor was in place as early as 1960, as noted by a reference to " the Belter Room," Dorothy Dawes Chillman to Ima Hogg, 20 July 1960, Ima Hogg Papers, Bayou Bend correspondence, MFAH Archives. A Belter Parlor is mentioned again in Progress Report from Bayou Bend, October 10, 1962, MFAH Archives. Ultimately, much of the mid-nineteenth-century furniture Miss Hogg collected found its way to the Governor's Mansion, her grandparents' home in Quitman, the Honeymoon Cottage, and Varner Plantation, as well as Bayou Bend.

43. The Thetas' initial gift is recorded in Bayou Bend Advisory Committee minutes, 11 February 1970, MFAH Archives. For a historical perspective, see Maura McCarthy, "50 Years of the Theta Charity Antiques Show," *50th Anniversary: Theta Charity Antiques Show* (Houston: Theta Charity Antiques Show, 2002), 28–33; see also the Museum of Fine Arts, Houston, *A Celebration of America's Past: The Theta Charity Antiques Show's Gifts to Bayou Bend* (Houston: The Museum of Fine Arts, Houston, 2002).

44. Bayou Bend Advisory Committee minutes, 3 April 1968. The following year, they made their initial gift to Bayou Bend. Bayou Bend Advisory Committee minutes, 14 May 1969, MFAH Archives.

45. Bayou Bend Advisory Committee minutes, 18 February 1975, MFAH Archives.

46. Bayou Bend Advisory Committee minutes, 6 February 1957, MFAH Archives.

47. Bayou Bend Advisory Committee minutes, 24 February 1960, MFAH Archives.

48. Ima Hogg to Vincent Andrus, 22 September 1952, Series 2: curatorial/American Wing, correspondence: Vincent Andrus, Metropolitan Museum of Art Archives.

49. Bayou Bend Advisory Committee minutes, 17 March 1981, MFAH Archives.

50. Ima Hogg to Ed Rotan and the Bayou Bend Advisory Committee, 12 August 1965, p. 3, MFAH Archives.

51. David B. Warren, "The Jordan Family of Georgia and Their Belter Parlor Furniture," *Antiques* 154, no. 6 (December 1998): 826–833.

52. Bayou Bend Advisory Committee minutes, 17 March 1981, MFAH Archives.

53. Charles F. Montgomery to Ima Hogg, 2 September 1960, Ima Hogg Papers, Bayou Bend renovations: consultants, 1960, MFAH Archives.

54. The Museum of Fine Arts, Houston, *One Great Night in November: A Twentieth Anniversary Celebration, 1984–2003* (Houston: The Museum of Fine Arts, Houston, 2003).

55. Collaborating with museum staff were Joseph Fronek, a paintings conservator from the Los Angeles County Museum of Art; Mary Ballard, from the Smithsonian Institution, who surveyed the textiles; Mark Anderson, Greg Landry, and Michael Podmaniczky, furniture conservators from the Winterthur Museum; and Andrew Lins, a conservator with the Philadelphia Museum of Art, who reviewed ceramics, glass, and metals.

56. Linda Baumgarten, from the Colonial Williamsburg Foundation, surveyed the textiles; Donald Fennimore, a Winterthur curator, reviewed the metals; and Jules Prown, a professor at Yale University, consulted on the paintings. Arlene Palmer Schwind studied the museum's ceramics and glass. Morrison Heckscher of the Metropolitan Museum of Art, surveyed the furniture. An extensive analysis of the cabinet woods was compiled by R. Bruce Hoadley of the University of Massachusetts, Amherst.

57. Ima Hogg to James Chillman, 20 December 1949, object file B.69.26, MFAH Archives.

58. Hart Galleries exhibition catalogue, *A Very Special Two-Day Auction: An Extensive Collection of Americana, Paintings, Folk Art, Decorations & Objects of Art, Deaccessioned from the Collection of Bayou Bend*, April 11 and 12, 1992, p. 2.

59. In 1963, Ima Hogg embarked on an ambitious restoration at Winedale, in the Texas Hill Country. There she assembled an extensive collection of furniture that reflected the traditions of the German immigrants who settled in the area. She went on to persuade Lonn Taylor and David Warren to research the genre, which resulted in their *Texas Furniture: The Cabinetmakers and Their Work, 1840–1880* (Austin: University of Texas Press, 1975). Another important publication was Cecilia Steinfeldt and Donald L. Stover, *Early Texas Furniture and Decorative Arts* (San Antonio: Trinity University Press, 1973).

60. Michael K. Brown, *The Wilson Potters: An African-American Enterprise in 19th-Century Texas* (Houston: The Museum of Fine Arts, Houston, 2002).

61. Warren, *Bayou Bend*, vii.

100 Masterpieces in the Bayou Bend Collection

1 Great Chair

1640–85
Essex County, Massachusetts

One object that had long appeared
on Ima Hogg's priority lists was a
great, or wainscot, chair. Though
more than half a century had passed
since one of these rare chairs entered
a public collection, by coincidence,
the two remaining in private hands
came to auction within months of
each other—one was acquired for the
Metropolitan Museum of Art and
the other for Bayou Bend. The latter
came from the distinguished collection formed by Bertram and Nina
Fletcher Little, avid collectors who
were friends of Miss Hogg's. Their
daughter, Selina, responding to
the museum's acquisition, wrote,
"I am delighted the chair has found
such a good home. My mother
always said that the best New England
antiques would end up, sooner or
later, in Texas."

White oak
37 5/8 x 23 1/2 x 20 3/4"
(95.6 x 59.7 x 52.7 cm)
Gift of Miss Ima Hogg by exchange
B.94.11

ℬℬ

2 *Posset Pot*

1628–51
Southwark, Montague Close,
or Pickleherring Pottery
London, England

In 1959, Ima Hogg enlisted her great friend and fellow collector Katharine Prentis Murphy to assist as she embarked upon creating a historic interior to display the earliest objects at Bayou Bend. Mrs. Murphy began making gifts for the room. When she sent down a pair of andirons, Miss Hogg protested, "Now, let us have an understanding about them at once! If they are to go into the room I am going to buy them! Please, Katharine, dear, don't embarrass me by giving me so many things. This room is to be in your honor and I can't think of having you supply the things which I would want to place there anyhow! It is my greatest pleasure!" Among the pieces Mrs. Murphy gave for the room was this rare, early London posset pot, which would become, and remains, the focal point of the British pottery in the museum's collection. Upon the interior's completion, Miss Hogg named it the Murphy Room in homage to her friend.

Tin-glazed earthenware
8 1/4 x 9 3/4 x 7 1/2" (21 x 24.8 x 19.1 cm)
Gift of Katharine Prentis Murphy
B.59.128

BB

3 Dish

c. 1685
London, England

Electra Havemeyer Webb was born
into a family of collectors. Her
parents, Horace and Louisine
Havemeyer, acquired Old Master
pictures, but they are best known for
being among the earliest and greatest
American patrons of the then avant-
garde Impressionists. By contrast,
Mrs. Webb was drawn to American
folk art and, over time, her collection
comprised paintings, sculpture,
and decorative arts, as well as toys,
horse-drawn vehicles, historic
buildings, a covered bridge, and the
steamboat *Ticonderoga*. Today, these
diverse collections are nestled into
a museum located on what was the
family farm at Shelburne, Vermont,
overlooking Lake Champlain. In
1957, when Miss Hogg donated
Bayou Bend to the Museum of Fine
Arts, Mrs. Webb offered this delftware
dish, with its ribald depiction. This
thoughtful gesture must have held
great significance for Miss Hogg,
because it affirmed her intent that
the collection at Bayou Bend would
attract the philanthropy of other,
like-minded donors.

Tin-glazed earthenware
2 3/8 x 13 11/16" (6 x 34.8 cm)
Gift of Mrs. J. Watson Webb
B.57.60

BB

4 Dram Cup

1655–64
Shop of John Hull (1624–1683)
and Robert Sanderson, Sr.
(1608–1693),
partnership 1652–83
Boston

Imagine the challenge of seeking major support for an object that is only an inch in height! The history of American silver begins with John Hull and Robert Sanderson, the earliest silversmiths whose work has come down to the present day. Many of their pieces are preserved as communion silver in churches throughout New England. The museum's dram cup, its name referring to a small draft of liquor, is among the handful of objects that remained in private hands. Keenly aware of its importance, its owner, whose father acquired it for his collection fifty years earlier, would only sell the diminutive vessel to a museum.

Silver
1 x 3 5/8 x 2 1/4" (2.5 x 9.2 x 5.7 cm)
Gift of the Theta Charity Antiques Show
B.96.8

5 Great Chair

1680–1700
South Carolina,
possibly Charleston

This imposing armchair is renowned as the earliest extant example of South Carolina furniture. Its maker may never be identified, but its design and distinctive components attest to a French influence. It probably represents the work of a Huguenot, or French Protestant, immigrant; in the seventeenth century, Huguenots accounted for a large percentage of South Carolina's population. The armchair, with its southern origin and early date, represented a major priority for Bayou Bend. When it was auctioned at Christie's in 1998, it achieved a record price for a southern armchair of this period.

Ash and black cherry
41 5/16 x 23 1/8 x 19"
(104.9 x 58.7 x 48.3 cm)
Gift of the Theta Charity Antiques Show
and, by exchange, Miss Ima Hogg,
Katharine Prentis Murphy,
Mr. and Mrs. Harris Masterson III,
Mrs. G. F. de Ridder, Mr. Jack McGregor,
and various other donors
B.98.19

6 Tankard

c. 1710
Shop of Peter Van Dyck
(1684–1751)
New York

In April 1967, Ralph Gibbs Whedon, Jr., first communicated with David Warren, then curator of the Bayou Bend Collection, hoping to locate the richly ornamented tankard made for his ancestors Thomas and Sarah Gibbs. The vessel, which his father sold in 1946, was acquired by Miss Hogg in 1953. Over the intervening years, the correspondence continued. It was proposed that Mr. Whedon consider giving to Bayou Bend his family papers from the 1840s that discussed the tankard, to which he countered: "We both appreciate the integrity of collections, but I would be happy to donate to Bayou Bend my entire Gibbs collection including an 1867 pewter mug, a 1770s silver watch (both with the Rich griffin) documents dating to the 1600s, letters 1770s to 1900, George Judson's various collections and writings, upon receipt from you of the Silver Tankard... Who could possibly detect a plated duplicate in your glass case?"

Ralph Gibbs Whedon, Jr.,
to Michael K. Brown
March 25, 1997

Silver
7 7/8 x 6 1/4 x 9 7/16" (20 x 15.9 x 24 cm)
Gift of Miss Ima Hogg
B.69.118

7 Tankard

1695–1711
Shop of John Coney
(1655/56–1722)
Boston

In the process of researching the collection, occasionally some personal recollections will surface, offering an extra dimension. One such instance is a 1984 note from Margaret Revere, a great-great-granddaughter of the patriot silversmith Paul Revere, which discusses the disposition of this silver tankard: " . . . Aunt Marion Revere left in her will that all her possessions should be divided by lot, after the death of her twin sister. This was done in December 1917. There were 18 lots to be drawn by the grandchildren of Mary Revere (Mrs. Joseph Warren Revere, mother of Marion). Cousin Jack (as we called him) drew in his lot the tankard. His brother Paul Revere Reynolds got a Paul Revere teapot. An uncle of mine got a bowl, unmarked, but attributed to Paul Revere, which I now own. Every lot had a P. R. tablespoon in it. Of course I didn't have any part in the drawing, though I was present. It was a most amusing occasion as after the heirs studied what they had gotten they swapped what they didn't want. In my family, this division was always known as 'The Great Divide.'"

Silver
6 15/16 x 5 1/16 x 8" (17.6 x 12.9 x 20.3 cm)
Gift of Miss Ima Hogg
B.74.19

8 Spoon

1678–1700
Shop of Jacob Boelen I
(c. 1657–1729)
New York

Silver flatware, in spite of encompass-ing seemingly inconspicuous objects, is a telling measure of stylistic changes in silver design as well as dining etiquette. Recognizing this, Miss Hogg included on her priority list a group of silver flatware "showing chronological development 17th to mid-19th century." Since the 1980s, important examples of flatware have been added to the collection. A spoon by Jeremiah Dummer, the earliest native-born silversmith whose work is known, introduces a survey that spans two centuries.

This particular type of spoon, noted for its distinctive cast handle, is a design first produced in Holland during the late sixteenth century. There, and among those of Dutch descent in colonial New York, it was reserved for holidays and family passages.

Silver
Length 6 1/2" (16.5 cm)
Gift of the William S. and
Lora Jean Kilroy Foundation
B.92.1

THE PINE ROOM, 1690–1760

9 Armchair

1730–40
Boston

At the time Miss Hogg was actively
collecting, early caned furniture
was not well understood and
presented scholars with a challenge
when trying to distinguish between
American and British examples.
When Miss Hogg was considering
this handsome chair, she enlisted
her advisor Jonathan Fairbanks to
travel to New York and examine it
for her. In looking back, Jonathan
freely admits that at the time he
could not be certain as to its origin,
but he believed in the chair and,
with his encouragement, she acquired
what has come to be recognized as
one of the preeminent American
expressions of this genre.

Soft maple; birch, cane
46 3/8 x 24 1/2 x 22"
(117.8 x 62.2 x 55.9 cm)
Gift of Miss Ima Hogg
B.61.40

10 High Chest of Drawers

1700–30
Boston

Ima Hogg recognized the William and Mary, or Early Baroque, high chest as the quintessential furniture form of the period. By 1953, when she began to consider this example, she already owned two others but questioned if they were of the quality she was trying to establish for the Bayou Bend Collection. Between May and July there was a brisk correspondence with her advisor Vincent Andrus:

"I can't resist the feminine last word about the William and Mary highboy at Walton's. I had glanced at it so hurriedly when I was in his shop that my impressions were vague, but spontaneous and without suggestions from anyone else. The only reason I had thought it was English at first was because of the veneering on the mouldings, which was unfamiliar to me in Wm & Mary American furniture. As soon as Walton sent the photographs I knew from the leg turnings that it was American, but I did not know; of course, how much of the period it was. I was very glad to hear from you concerning it. It will be interesting to see if you think the one I have is any good. I really need a fine one, and perhaps a matching lowboy. Maybe you know where they are."

Ima Hogg to
Vincent D. Andrus
June 20, 1953

Black walnut, burled walnut veneer,
brass; aspen, birch, eastern white pine,
hemlock, soft maple
68 1/4 x 40 1/4 x 22 1/4"
(173.4 x 102.2 x 56.5 cm)
Gift of Miss Ima Hogg
B.69.43

11 Tall Clock

1725–46
Movement by Peter Stretch (1670–1746)
Case attributed to John Head (1688–1754)
Philadelphia

Those interested in clocks can be divided into two groups. Some concentrate on the clockmaker and movement, while others focus on aesthetics which, for the most part, center on the case. Peter Stretch, one of the earliest clockmakers documented to ply his craft in the colony, and other early Philadelphia clockmakers have not until recently attracted the same attention as their New England contemporaries. Collectors have tended to focus on the latter region, based on past preferences, scholarship, and the fact that New England clock cases tend to be more developed, with the occasional burl veneered and japanned surfaces, versus a solid black walnut facade. The Bayou Bend tall clock affirms this predilection. When the museum purchased this clock in 1986, the only other major art museum with a Stretch clock in its collection was the Philadelphia Museum of Art.

Black walnut, brass, glass; Atlantic white cedar, eastern white pine, southern yellow pine, brass, iron
103 x 20 3/8 x 10 5/8" (261.6 x 51.8 x 27 cm)
Gift of the Theta Charity Antiques Show in memory of Betty Black Hatchett B.86.4

Samuel Pemberton · JOHN SMIBERT, 1688-1751 · American School

12 *Portrait of Samuel Pemberton*

1734
John Smibert (1688–1751)
Boston

In the 1950s, when Miss Hogg decided to transform her home into a house museum, she began collecting in other media, such as painting, to enrich the picture of American culture that she had created at Bayou Bend. She claimed, with characteristic modesty, that she was not putting together a definitive collection but, rather, "a few portraits as accessories, or background" when opportunities presented themselves. Her collection of American paintings at Bayou Bend is, of course, far more than that. Among the liveliest paintings in the collection is this distinguished portrait of a bewigged eleven-year-old boy from Boston, Samuel Pemberton, presented in its original Baroque carved frame. Scottish-born John Smibert was the first major art celebrity in the American colonies. He painted at least four other members of the wealthy Pemberton family, including an older brother, James (unlocated), Samuel's sister Hannah (Metropolitan Museum of Art), and Mary, also acquired by Miss Hogg in 1972.
EBN

Oil on canvas; original eastern white pine frame
30 1/8 x 25 1/2" (76.5 x 64.8 cm)
Gift of Miss Ima Hogg
B.72.7

13 Card Table

1730–60
Boston

When this card table came to light in 1951, it was understood to have been made for Peter Faneuil (1700–1743), the Boston merchant who gave his city the now-historic hall that bears his name. The table is a great rarity—the frame is inlaid, the sides designed so when the top is closed they would fold into the back, but most remarkable of all is its needlework top. Furthermore, it was reported that a mate existed, making them the earliest pair of American card tables known. As time has passed, it is now difficult to prove the tables belonged to Faneuil—his household inventory does not record a pair of card tables. However, they did descend through the family of his sister, Mary Ann Jones. Did she inherit the tables, or were they commissioned for her? Perhaps she worked their embroidered tops, which are now believed to be the second cover: textile scholars point out that tambour work was not produced much earlier than 1770. In spite of this scholarly reassessment, the Faneuil card table remains one of Bayou Bend's enduring masterpieces.

Mahogany, unidentified inlay, brass, wool; cherry, eastern white pine, mahogany, spruce
Open: 26 3/4 x 37 x 32 1/8" (67.9 x 94 x 81.6 cm)
Closed: 27 1/4 x 36 1/4 x 18" (69.2 x 92.1 x 48.3 cm)
Gift of Miss Ima Hogg
B.69.406

14 *Portrait of Mrs. Matthew Tilghman and Her Daughter, Anna Maria*

c. 1757
John Hesselius (1728–1778)
Chestertown, Maryland

The question of eighteenth-century attributions is an ongoing study in the field of American art. For example, it was not until the 1980s that a portrait Miss Hogg had acquired in 1960 as a work by John Hesselius, a major portraitist of the mid-Atlantic colonies and an early mentor to the celebrated Charles Willson Peale, was reattributed as an early work by an English painter. In accordance with Miss Hogg's wishes that the collection continue to be upgraded according to the result of new research and opportunities, Bayou Bend staff continuously combed the market for a suitable replacement. This rare double portrait of a distinguished Maryland mother and daughter, in whose family it descended, came on the market at a perfect time: when David B. Warren retired after a thirty-eight-year career as Bayou Bend's first curator and director. With funds provided by two of Bayou Bend's most loyal patrons, the Theta Charity Antiques Show and The Brown Foundation, Inc., this elegant and aristocratic portrait by Hesselius was acquired in David Warren's honor.
EBN

Oil on linen
48 3/8 x 38 1/2" (122.9 x 97.8 cm)
Gift of the Theta Charity Antiques Show and
The Brown Foundation, Inc., in honor of
David B. Warren
B.2003.6

15 Portrait of Mrs. Samuel McCall, Sr.

1746
Robert Feke (c. 1707–1751)
Philadelphia

In collecting, restraint can be a virtue. Miss Hogg was eager to acquire a work by Robert Feke, the first major native-born artist of the British North American colonies. David Warren, then Bayou Bend's curator, encouraged her to pass on an inferior one and wait for a major example. In 1971, this large portrait, one of several extant portraits of Philadelphia's McCall family, was offered to Bayou Bend. It was worth the wait. Miss Hogg acquired from the sitter's descendants the painting of a young Philadelphia lady, posed in the manner of a well-known 1737 portrait of Queen Caroline of England by Joseph Highmore and engraved by John Faber. Imposing, elegant, and spare, this portrait by Feke shows how the artist provided dignified portraits for his clientele, whether in Newport, Boston, Virginia, Barbados, or Philadelphia.
EBN

Oil on canvas
49 7/8 x 39 7/8" (126.7 x 101.3 cm)
Gift of Miss Ima Hogg
B.71.81

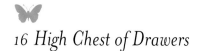

16 High Chest of Drawers

1730-60
Boston

Shortly after New Year's 1955, Miss Hogg acquired this Boston high chest, resplendent with its japanned facade, from dealer John Walton. It arrived with an impressive pedigree, having been published by Joseph Downs and been on loan to the Society for the Preservation of New England Antiquities (SPNEA, now Historic New England). Before the chest was purchased, her advisor Vincent Andrus expressed to Miss Hogg and the dealer his reservations about the condition of the decoration. Walton disagreed and elaborated on his invoice, "The original japanning has been touched up, restored in parts and varnished with spar varnish to preserve." Months later, correspondence reveals that Miss Hogg was beginning to have second thoughts about the piece. She wrote Andrus, "I regret to say that I am very fond of this highboy, but I certainly would not wish to offer it to our Museum if it were embarrassing in any way to them." With help from Andrus and Walton, she assembled an impressive dossier which included correspondence from the previous owner and SPNEA director Bertram Little, reaffirming the condition of the decoration. Andrus subsequently revised his original assessment:

"In regard to the highboy, I had meant to write you after a recent visit to Winterthur. One of their japanned highboys of which they are very proud would appear to be in the same condition as yours. As you write, how much new work has been done would appear to be important but very difficult to determine. All in all I think you should feel that it deserves a place in the museum. There will probably never be an opportunity to get another."

Paint, gesso, gold leaf, eastern white pine,
soft maple, brass; eastern white pine
87 x 41 1/2 x 23" (221 x 105.4 x 58.4 cm)
Gift of Miss Ima Hogg
B.69.348

17 Chocolate Pot

1750–65
Staffordshire, England

Collecting interests are typically shaped by education and exposure, as well as taste and curiosity. A case in point is the extensive collection of ceramics that Miss Hogg formed, comprising more than 1,500 objects. Although she acquired American porcelains and pottery as well as Chinese export porcelain, it was British pottery of the seventeenth and eighteenth centuries that was her principle passion. Perhaps her partiality can be credited, in part, to her visits to Colonial Williamsburg in the 1950s. There, through her friendship with John Graham, its chief curator, and by attending the institution's Antiques Forums, she benefited from unusual access to the collection. She was drawn to delft, salt-glazed stoneware, mottled glazed wares, and agate wares, and these predominate in her collection. Agate wares, with their variegated colored clay producing a marbleized appearance, must have held a special appeal. In time, she assembled close to a dozen examples, including this chocolate pot fashioned in a bold Baroque contour.

Lead-glazed earthenware
9 x 5 7/8 x 4 3/4" (22.9 x 14.9 x 12.1 cm)
Gift of Miss Ima Hogg
B.56.107

18 Teapot

1728–48
Shop of Bartholomew Schaats
(1670–1758)
New York

Individuals' response to the same object can be totally subjective. In October 1953, Miss Hogg was considering this simple, spherical teapot bearing the stamp of Bartholomew Schaats. Miss Hogg's advisor Vincent Andrus examined the vessel and offered his candid appraisal: "The Schaats' teapot is early but my personal preference is for a flush cover on this type of pot. This high cover seems a bit awkward, although the design is very rare in American pots." Miss Hogg felt otherwise and, contrary to Andrus's counsel, decided to acquire it. The Bayou Bend teapot is one of only six known and, in 1980, the Metropolitan Museum purchased one of the other five, an example by Benjamin Wynkoop, Jr., that is virtually identical to this one by Schaats.

Silver, unidentified wood
6 1/2 x 4 3/4 x 9 13/16" (16.5 x 12.1 x 24.9 cm)
Gift of Miss Ima Hogg
B.69.111

19 Cream Pot

1745–55
Shop of Jacob Hurd (1702/3–1758)
Boston

With the exception of porringers, the cream pot was the most prevalent holloware form in the silversmith's inventory. The vast majority are simple objects, usually devoid of any decoration. Antiques dealer Albert Sack recounts that Miss Hogg visited his shop and was smitten by this pot. It is one of a handful of examples embellished with engraved scenes implying the advantages of pastoral life that embody the spirit of the Rococo. Though obviously infatuated by it, Miss Hogg observed a solder joint just below the lip and asked if it was a repair. Sack, being a furniture man, was unable to supply a definitive answer, so he consulted with Charles Montgomery and learned that it is a construction peculiar to Boston where the spout is not integral but formed separately from the body and then attached.

Silver
4 1/16 x 2 1/2 x 3 1/2" (10.3 x 6.4 x 8.9 cm)
Gift of Miss Ima Hogg
B.69.112

20 *Tea Caddy*

1728–33
Shop of Simeon Soumain
(1685–1750)
New York

"I am not really anxious to sell the tea caddy as I would like to keep it for our own collection. Actually, they are such small things and of such rare and collectible quality, that I feel a collector can make a decision without trying them first. But I always seem to bow to the wishes of Miss Hogg."

Bernard Levy of Ginsburg & Levy Inc., to Jane Zivley, secretary to Miss Hogg
September 13, 1962

"Thanks for your letter of September 13. Under the circumstances, I think all I would like to have you send me at the present time is the tea caddy. I hope to be up in New York this autumn and, while I do not need much of anything, I would love to be *tempted!* In the meantime, let me hear of anything 'special.'"

Ima Hogg to Bernard Levy
September 19, 1962

Silver
5 3/16 x 3 5/16 x 2 1/2" (13.2 x 13.5 x 6.4 cm)
Gift of Miss Ima Hogg
B.62.38

21 Tea Table

1740–90
Boston

Boldly executed Boston tea tables have long been prized. The distinctive "turret" top and contoured skirt rails combine to make this table one of the more dynamic creations. The shaped rim was devised to secure the tea service, and the semicircular scalloping framed the teacups and saucers. In fact, by 1961, four of the five known examples were in the collections of Henry Francis du Pont, Henry and Helen Flynt, Maxim Karolik, and Miss Hogg, all of them destined for museum collections. A decade earlier, at Miss Hogg's behest, antiques dealer Israel Sack traveled to Michigan to examine this superb example. If he thought it was period and endorsed its condition, he was to purchase it on her behalf. The table surpassed his expectations and has been a focal point of the Massachusetts Room ever since.

Mahogany; no secondary woods intact
27 3/4 x 32 1/8 x 23 5/8" (70.5 x 81.6 x 60 cm)
Gift of Miss Ima Hogg
B.69.362

22 *Looking Glass*

Looking Glass
1730–60
Probably Boston

Looking glasses, more than any other
furniture form, present unique challenges to the connoisseur. As such,
they are the least understood group
of American furniture. Documentary
evidence confirms that the majority
found in the colonies were British or
Continental imports; early American
glassmakers did not possess the skills
or facilities to produce sheets of glass
of sufficient smoothness and clarity
for silvering. Microscopic analysis of
the wooden frames helps to distinguish between American and foreign
examples. The presence of eastern
white pine on the museum's frame
provides the basis for its American
attribution. However, were the
piece later in date, there would be
no assurances that it was of domestic
manufacture. By 1803, in discussing
the attributes of American eastern
white pine, Thomas Sheraton
observed, "Within fifty years past,
they have been planted in Great
Britain in considerable plenty."

Paint, mirrored glass; eastern white pine
17 1/2 x 9 3/8 x 1 3/8 (44.5 x 23.8 x 3.5 cm)
Gift of The Brown Foundation, Inc.,
in honor of David B. Warren
B.2001.5

23 Portrait of Mrs. Richard Nicholls

1749
John Wollaston (active 1742–75)
New York

This striking portrait by John Wollaston, a prolific and celebrated artist throughout parts of the British North American colonies and the West Indies, likely descended with three portraits by John Singleton Copley in a family of colonial Loyalists who returned to England. Thus, it is not surprising that this New York matron—illuminated by dramatic light and dressed in shimmering silks contrasted with sharply defined, crisp lace—should turn up in a London art gallery. There it was acquired by Houston collector Harris Masterson, who eventually, inspired by the model of Bayou Bend, established his home, Rienzi, as a wing of the Museum of Fine Arts, Houston, specializing in European decorative arts and painting. Mr. Masterson's gift of this portrait to Bayou Bend continued the tradition begun by Katharine Prentis Murphy and Electra Havemeyer Webb of enriching Bayou Bend's collection in honor of the friendships that developed through the pursuit of their passion to preserve cultural history. EBN

Oil on canvas
30 x 25" (76.2 x 63.5 cm)
Gift of Mr. and Mrs. Harris Masterson III
in memory of Libbie Johnston Masterson
B. 69.344

THE DRAWING ROOM, 1760–90

24 Side Chair

1750–75
New York

In the 1750s and 1760s, Britain's
aristocrats, furniture designers, and
craftsmen collaborated to produce
suites of furniture with pierced backs
that incorporated the intertwining
initials of their prominent patrons.
In America, the fashion hardly caught
on; in fact, the only known instance
of this device being adopted is a set
of eight side chairs with the initials
RML. The uniqueness of this group
made it particularly appealing to
private and institutional collectors.
One would think that by employing
this personal device, the provenance
would be easily determined. However,
in this instance, three successive
generations of Robert Livingstons
married women named Margaret,
Margaret, and Mary, respectively.
The actual identification was only
resolved thanks to the survival of a
nineteenth-century needlework seat
cover with the initials for Catherine
Livingston Garretson, thereby ascrib-
ing the chairs to her parents, Robert
and Margaret Beekman Livingston,
the second generation.

Mahogany, beech; cherry,
eastern white pine, yellow-poplar
41 1/2 x 22 1/2 x 21 1/2" (105.4 x 57.2 x 54.6 cm)
Gift of Miss Ima Hogg
B.69.33

25 Roundabout Chair

1750–1800
New York

Boston, Newport, and Philadelphia
furniture have always generated more
attention than examples from the
New York school—as evidenced by
the Bayou Bend Collection.
Although Miss Hogg acquired some
important eighteenth-century New
York pieces, the museum's holdings
are modest by comparison to those
from the three other urban centers.
Included in this select group is
this roundabout chair, a fully developed example distinguished by its
foliate-carved knee ornament and
its graceful cabriole legs that echo
the contours of the supports for
the back and arms. Its provenance
is unknown, but a clue exists in
the distinctive knee ornament.
This highly unusual device was
also employed on a pair of side
chairs believed to have been owned
by General Philip Schuyler, suggesting that the roundabout chair was
his as well.

Mahogany; mahogany, yellow pine
32 x 32 1/4 x 25 1/4" (81.3 x 81.9 x 64.1 cm)
Gift of Miss Ima Hogg
B.69.401

ℬℬ
26 Bureau Table

1760–1800
Newport or possibly Providence

The American furniture market attained a new level in January 1986, when a Philadelphia Rococo tea table realized slightly more than one million dollars at auction. Three years later, a Newport desk-and-bookcase brought more than twelve million dollars, setting a record that has stood for nearly two decades. Over the intervening years, almost fifty pieces of early American furniture have sold for seven figures, and the competition is largely dominated by examples from the Philadelphia and Newport schools. Richly conceived and executed Philadelphia pieces emulated British fashion, whereas Newport furniture is celebrated for its restrained, innovative design, precise construction details, and selection of boldly figured mahogany that otherwise is rarely encountered in eighteenth-century America. An iconic form is the bureau table with its contrasting convex, concave robustly carved Baroque shells, heralded as America's most significant contribution to eighteenth-century design. This example is distinguished by its provenance, having descended from John Brown, the immensely wealthy Providence merchant, and its configuration—its top drawer being sectioned for use as a dressing table.

Mahogany, brass; chestnut, eastern white pine, mahogany, soft maple, yellow-poplar, cedrela odorata
31 1/2 x 36 3/4 x 20 3/4" (80 x 93.3 x 52.7 cm)
Gift of Mr. and Mrs. James L. Britton, Jr.
B.92.6

27 *Card Table*

1760–90
Newport

There are a variety of motivations for attaching the name of an artist or artisan to an object. Such an association can have a significant impact on its value, and can contribute to its identification and interpretation. More than once it has been suggested that this important Newport card table is the work of John Goddard, largely because of the fact that it was made for Thomas Robinson, whose residence was only four blocks from Goddard's home and adjoining cabinet shop. Sometimes the effort to associate a piece with a maker can become so all-consuming that the object itself can become secondary—but not in this instance. The museum's table represents an unconventional commission and, therefore, one of the most unusual pieces to emanate from Newport.

Mahogany, brass; eastern white pine, white oak, and maple
Open: 25 1/2 x 35 1/8 x 35"
(64.8 x 89.2 x 88.9 cm)
Closed: 25 1/2 x 35 1/8 x 17 3/8
(64.8 x 89.2 x 44.1 cm)
Gift of the Estate of Marian M. Britton
B.99.25

28 Bureau Table

1785–1800
Attributed to the shop of John Townsend
(1732/33–1809)
Newport

With eleven of the twelve Rhode Island block-front desk-and-book-cases secured in public collections (including Bayou Bend), collectors such as Miss Hogg and the Brittons (cat. 26) who wished to acquire block and shell furniture have turned to the bureau table, a related form that is more prevalent. In October 1946, Miss Hogg engaged dealer Israel Sack in her quest. He brought this superb example to her attention but explained that its owner, Mrs. George C. Kellogg, in whose family it had descended, had no interest in selling and intended to leave it to her nephew. Sack would contact him, but was quite certain that negotiations could not transpire as long as Mrs. Kellogg was still living. Sack wrote to Miss Hogg, "You have my assurance that I will do my very best to have you get the desk if it is at all possible. I have learned from experience with all these very superior pieces of furniture that a lot of patience is required

under such circumstances. All the fine old furniture that was made in this country from 1600–1800 or any other country for that matter was built with great patience, and it requires patience to acquire the fine things."

In July 1950, Miss Hogg was abroad when Sack reached her with the news that Mrs. Kellogg had died and the bureau table would be offered through a process of sealed bids. A flurry of communications between New York, Amsterdam, Paris, and London followed. Patience had indeed paid off, and the two prevailed.

Mahogany, brass; chestnut, yellow-poplar
34 1/2 x 39 1/4 x 22"
(87.6 x 99.7 x 55.9 cm)
Gift of Miss Ima Hogg
B.69.91

29 *Desk-and-Bookcase*

1755–1800
Newport

Albert Sack, the dean of American antiques dealers, recalls an amusing anecdote about this great desk-and-bookcase, which is closely related to the Newport desks incorporating six carved shells. In the 1920s, this example was discovered in Rhode Island. An antiques dealer from New York made arrangements to see the desk-and-bookcase, owned by a local dealer. The New York dealer coveted it, but lest he betray his enthusiasm, he added the quip, "Too bad about that Victorian finial," to which the local dealer tersely responded, "Yep, too bad." The New York dealer then inquired about the price and negotiated the purchase for $19,000. After the desk was loaded on his truck, he discovered the finial was missing and questioned its whereabouts. The local dealer responded, "Well, you don't want that Victorian finial, do you?" A thousand dollars later, the "Victorian" finial was reunited with the desk and en route to New York.

Mahogany; chestnut,
eastern white pine, yellow-poplar
98 1/4 x 43 3/8 x 25 1/2"
(249.6 x 110.2 x 64.8 cm)
Gift of the Estate of Marian M. Britton
B.99.24

30 *Slab Table*

1760–1800
Philadelphia

Dealer Harold Sack recounts the discovery of this Philadelphia masterpiece. The owner's high estimation of his table was evident by the price he was asking. The Sacks struggled with the amount. In order to justify the purchase, they would have to raise the market to a new level. Later, people were aghast at what they were asking—as Sack observed, "We had many visitors and browsers to see the table, but no buyers." Miss Hogg stopped by and though she was duly impressed, she could not reconcile the price. A few weeks later, she invited Harold to visit her at Bayou Bend, suggesting he help evaluate the collection to ensure that her objects were of museum quality. The morning after his arrival, she asked how he had slept. He responded that he was unable to sleep a wink—he was up the entire night trying to think of how he might sell her the table. She laughed, and agreed with his contention that it belonged with the other great furniture she had assembled in Philadelphia Hall. Eventually they settled on a price. Afterward, she would often exclaim, "Oh, Harold, I'm so glad you made me buy that table! Your father would have done exactly the same thing!"

Mahogany, marble; southern yellow pine, white oak, yellow-poplar
29 1/2 x 49 7/8 x 22 1/2" (74.9 x 126.7 x 57.2 cm)
Gift of Miss Ima Hogg
B.59.82

31 *Portrait of a Boy*

c. 1758–60
John Singleton Copley (1738–1815)
Boston

In 1954, Miss Hogg acquired her
first painting by John Singleton
Copley, more than a decade before
the major retrospective exhibition
and catalogue of Copley's career that
definitively established him as one
of the great eighteenth-century
painters of any nationality. As told
by Boston art dealer Robert C. Vose,
Miss Hogg acted quickly. At the
moment he secured the painting
from former Massachusetts governor
Alvan T. Fuller, he called Miss Hogg,
only to learn that she was staying at
the historic Red Lion Inn in
Stockbridge, Massachusetts. When
he called her at the inn, she agreed
to see the painting and immediately
purchased it on the spot, even
though the dealer mispronounced
her name "Hoag." This bold, early
work by one of America's greatest
masters was an astute purchase and
beautifully conveys the hallmarks of
Copley's early style. Characterized
by strong color, theatrical lighting,
and attention to fine detail, Copley
surrounds this jaunty boy with a
profusion of props—the signs of
privilege, wealth, and social standing
expected of aristocratic eighteenth-
century portraiture.
EBN

Oil on canvas; original gilded, eastern white pine frame
48 5/8 x 36 1/4" (123.5 x 92.1 cm)
Gift of Miss Ima Hogg
B.54.31

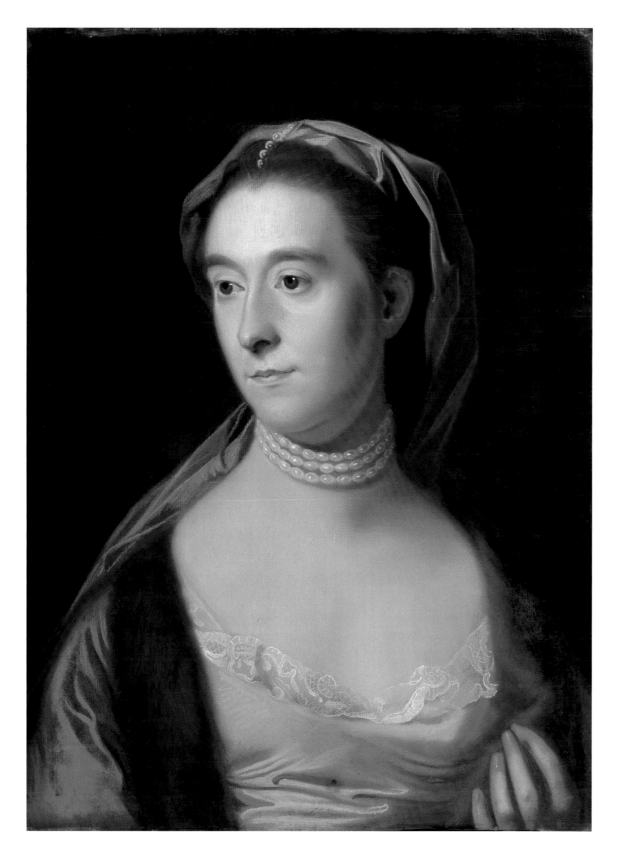

Pastel on paper, mounted on linen
24 x 17 3/4" (61 x 45.1 cm)
Gift of Miss Ima Hogg
B.54.25

32 Portrait of Mrs. Joseph Henshaw

c. 1770
John Singleton Copley (1738–1815)
Boston

With antiques dealer Bernard Levy bidding on her behalf, Miss Hogg secured two Copley pastels, including this exquisite one, at the celebrated auction of the late Mr. and Mrs. Luke Vincent Lockwood at Parke-Bernet in 1954. Miss Hogg recognized the superior artistic skill of this major American figure and ultimately acquired a total of ten Copleys in a variety of media. But this major pastel, painted when Copley was at the height of his refinement in this difficult medium, almost got away. Another renowned collector of Americana, Henry Flynt, tried unsuccessfully to acquire this work, which portrays his distant relative. Learning of this, Miss Hogg wrote a letter to Mr. Flynt chastising him for not overbidding in order to secure it and at the same time offering to exchange hers for another so he could have it. Mr. Flynt, collecting for what is now Historic Deerfield, was charmed by Miss Hogg's offer and wrote, "Your thoughtful letter delighted Helen [his wife] and me tremendously. It is just another manifestation of your graciousness and bears out what we have always felt—that you are a truly great lady in the finest sense of the word." Miss Hogg must have been greatly relieved when she received his response. As she wrote to Mr. Levy, "I have just received a lovely letter from Mr. Flynt assuring me that he is happy for me to have the Copley portrait of Sarah Henshaw. Of course, you know I am very pleased as I had really wanted [it]."
EBN

33 *Punch Bowl*

c. 1770–80
China

Henry Francis du Pont was passionate
about Chinese export porcelain.
Between 1923, when he began collecting, and 1951, when he opened
Winterthur, he had amassed a
collection numbering more than
five thousand pieces. By comparison,
while Miss Hogg's Chinese porcelains were equally choice, they were
far fewer in number. Included
among them is this early punch bowl
depicting the Hongs—the offices and
living quarters rented by the overseas
trading firms in Canton. Bowls such
as this one have long been highly
prized; in fact, they are seemingly
requisite to a great American collection. While many collectors would
have insisted on one brandishing an
American flag, Miss Hogg's example,
with flags representing the French
and Honourable East India
Company, is an earlier and far
rarer vessel.

Hard-paste porcelain
6 5/8 x 15 3/4" (16.8 x 40 cm)
Gift of Miss Ima Hogg
B.67.1

BB

34 *Europe, Asia, America, and Africa: The Four Corners of the Globe*

1770–80
Chelsea or Chelsea-Derby
England

In 1990, President George H. W. Bush hosted heads of state Margaret Thatcher, François Mitterand, Helmut Kohl, Brian Mulroney, Giulio Andreotti, Toshiki Kaifu, and Jacques Delors for a dinner at Bayou Bend during the Economic Summit of Industrialized Nations. In an effort to be historically relevant, and in the spirit of international cooperation, this quartet of cherubic porcelain figures were stationed about the dining table in a manner consistent with eighteenth-century etiquette. Representing the continents Europe, Asia, America, and Africa, they provided the perfect complement when this august group of world leaders came to dinner at Bayou Bend.

Soft-paste porcelain
Europe: 9 x 4 1/2 x 4 1/4"
(22.9 x 11.5 x 10.8 cm)
Asia: 8 3/4 x 4 7/8 x 4 1/8"
(22.3 x 12.4 x 10.5 cm)
America: 8 3/4 x 4 5/8 x 4 1/4"
(22.3 x 11.8 x 10.8 cm)
Africa: 8 7/8 x 4 3/8 x 4 1/4"
(22.6 x 11.2 x 10.8 cm)
Gift of Mrs. Fred T. Couper, Jr.,
in loving memory of her mother,
Mrs. William Victor Bowles
B.87.1.1–.4

35 Chest-on-Chest

1760–1800
Philadelphia

The dispersal of Howard Reifsnyder's renowned collection in 1929 remains one of the landmark auctions of eighteenth-century American furniture. A record price was established when Henry Francis du Pont prevailed over William Randolph Hearst to purchase the Philadelphia Rococo high chest, which came down in the Van Pelt family, for $44,000. At the same sale, this Philadelphia chest-on-chest realized $29,000. Ima and Will Hogg were well aware of the Reifsnyder sale but did not participate. Two decades later, having passed through two private collections, the chest-on-chest was back on the market and this time Miss Hogg was keenly interested. She wrote to her advisor Vincent Andrus in 1951, "It was so kind of you to come to Ginsburg and Levy and give me the benefit of your advice. I enjoyed so much looking at the pieces through your eyes. As I told you on the phone, I saw the Reifsnyder chest on chest anew and went back to the hotel feeling like I wanted to make a desperate effort to purchase it. I told Mr. Levy I would take it."

Mahogany, brass; Atlantic white cedar, mahogany, southern yellow pine, white oak, yellow-poplar
92 1/2 x 47 1/8 x 23 3/4" (235 x 119.7 x 60.3 cm)
Gift of Miss Ima Hogg
B.69.74

36 *High Chest of Drawers*

c. 1760–1800
Philadelphia

Mahogany, brass; Atlantic white cedar, cedar,
mahogany, southern yellow pine, yellow-poplar
94 3/8 x 46 1/2 x 30 5/8" (239.7 x 118.1 x 77.8 cm)
Gift of Miss Ima Hogg
B.69.75

Among American furniture collectors, the Philadelphia high chest of drawers is universally recognized as an icon, due to its scale and architectonic form, the robustness and depth of the Rococo carving, and its uniqueness as an American expression—the high chest was long out of fashion in Britain but persisted in colonial America. The Bayou Bend example first came to light in 1935 when William MacPherson Hornor, Jr., published it in the *Blue Book, Philadelphia Furniture, William Penn to George Washington*. Hornor dedicated a full page to its illustration and wrote, "In Every Respect This Highboy from the Wharton Family Mansion is Faultless. It May be Said That This One is Unsurpassed by Any Philadelphia-Chippendale Highboy Remaining in a Colonial Family." In 1952 the descendants who had inherited the chest began to consider how they might dispose of it, and it was not long before the word was out. Two antiques dealers contacted Miss Hogg, each offering to represent her but, unbeknownst to them, she had already quietly entered into negotiations for it. Once it had been sold, she received an inquiry from a third, Israel Sack: "We heard through the grapevine that somebody in Texas bought the Wharton Lisle highboy for $30,000.00. Of course, we are curious to know if you know the party who purchased it. You know, we get some very fine American items occasionally and are always looking for new recruits to the cause of Americana."

37 *Portrait of Mrs. Paul Richard*

1771
John Singleton Copley (1738–1815)
New York

This London-born heiress married
Paul Richard, a wealthy importer and
mayor of New York City, but had
been widowed fifteen years when
Copley painted her portrait in 1771.
This striking painting is the only
dowager portrait among a rare group
of portraits Copley painted during a
seven-month stay in New York while
his grand home atop Boston's
Beacon Hill was being refurbished
and expanded. At this time in his
career, Copley simplified his compositions in order to heighten the
psychological complexity of his sitters. Here, seventy-one-year-old
Mrs. Richard displays the signs of
age: puffy hands, shadowed face,
worn with deep crevices, knotted
brow, protruding lower lip, and
piercing eyes—all closely observed
details that enhance the lifelike
qualities of the portrait. Mrs.
Richard may not have been among
New York's celebrated beauties,
but she seems to have been deeply
treasured by her husband, who
once described her as "my all and
Second Selfe."
EBN

Oil on canvas
50 x 39 1/2" (127 x 100.3 cm)
Gift of Miss Ima Hogg
B.54.18

38 Armchair

1763–71
Philadelphia

In 1959, this stately armchair from Arthur Sussel's collection was to be auctioned at Parke-Bernet. John Walton, who had sold a number of masterworks to Miss Hogg, wrote that it was coming up and offered to represent her.

After attending his first auction in 1921, Miss Hogg's brother Will conceded to her, "Although I got excellent examples of the articles purchased I am prone to believe that I might have done better buying from a dealer—even the favored one on Madison Avenue." Perhaps recalling her brother's comment, by the 1940s, as Miss Hogg resumed collecting, she confided she was "awfully afraid of auctions." Aside from the Sussel sale, the only other time Miss Hogg purchased at auction was when Luke Vincent Lockwood's celebrated collection was dispersed by Parke-Bernet in 1954.

Mahogany; white oak
40 3/4 x 28 3/8 x 28 1/2"
(103.5 x 72.1 x 72.4 cm)
Gift of Miss Ima Hogg
B.60.30

39 *Easy Chair*

1750–1800
Eastern Massachusetts

About the time that Bayou Bend was dedicated to the public in 1966, Miss Hogg reflected upon her years of collecting: "I never felt that anything here belonged to me. I always bought with the idea that everything would one day go to a museum." Unique among the many masterpieces in the collection is this eastern Massachusetts easy chair, recognized as one of the most highly prized survivals among eighteenth-century upholstered furniture—only two others, at the Metropolitan Museum of Art and Winterthur, have come down with their original needlework covers. At the time Miss Hogg acquired the chair, she conceded she was also assuming responsibility to be its steward—as is evident in a letter she wrote to Ernest LoNano, who was going to work on the chair for her: "Now, on the advice of Mr. Charles Montgomery, we feel it best not to take the covering off the chair, but cleaning it and mending only those places which are urgently needed."

Mahogany, original wool show cover;
birch, soft maple, unidentified secondary woods,
original upholstery foundation
45 1/2 x 32 3/4 x 31 3/4"
(115.6 x 83.2 x 80.6 cm)
Gift of Miss Ima Hogg
B.60.89

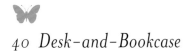

40 Desk-and-Bookcase

1780–1800
Boston

The appearance of objects can change over time. Thomas Dawes's architectonic desk-and-bookcase, a masterpiece of late eighteenth-century Boston furniture, descended through five successive generations of his family until 1954 when it was acquired by antiques dealer David Stockwell. Having determined that the finial and hardware were replacements, he restored it to what he believed was its original appearance. Later that year, Miss Hogg purchased the desk, and so it remained for almost fifty years. More recently, a photograph of it taken about 1940 prompted a reexamination by curators and conservators; based on the information it imparted, when combined with physical evidence and scholarship, the finial and hardware were changed out once again—all in that never-ending quest to recapture the desk's original appearance from two centuries earlier.

Mahogany, brass, mirrored glass;
eastern white pine
94 5/8 x 40 x 21 3/8"
(240.3 x 101.6 x 54.3 cm)
Gift of Miss Ima Hogg
B.69.139

41 *Dressing Glass*

1750–90
Boston

In addition to seeking out potential acquisitions, a curator's related responsibility is identifying a donor who will respond to the object. One of the more memorable instances was when this diminutive bombé dressing glass came on the market. Bombé furniture is admired for its dynamic contour and it comprises the most ambitious group of eighteenth-century Massachusetts case pieces. Ima Hogg recognized its importance, as evidenced by two Boston desk-and-bookcases (cat. 40) and a Salem chest of drawers she collected. The dressing glass is the rarest of all bombé forms. Who could not respond to this beguiling miniature? The piece was sent to Bayou Bend on approval and displayed on top of the bombé chest. The prospective donor, Mrs. Anderson immediately recognized its significance and was so overwhelmed that she asked if she could have a chair to sit down. The following morning she telephoned to say she would be pleased to underwrite the acquisition.

Mahogany, brass, mirrored glass;
eastern white pine
27 1/8 x 19 x 8 3/16" (68.9 x 48.3 x 22.4 cm)
Gift of Mrs. James Anderson, Jr.
B.2001.6

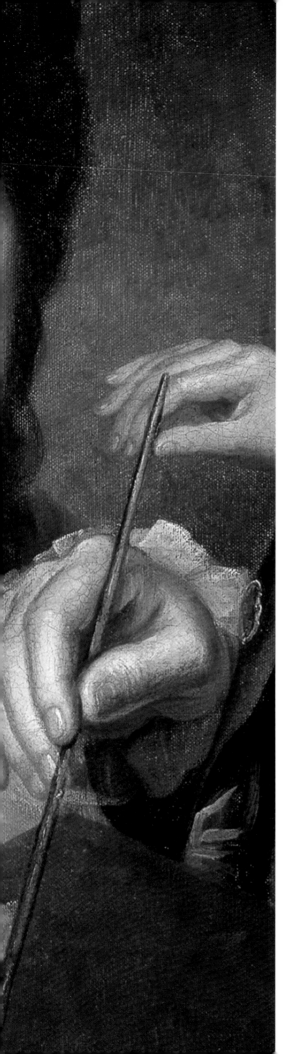

42 Miniature Portrait of a Young Boy

c. 1768
Charles Willson Peale (1741–1827)
Philadelphia

Miniatures, or "painting in little," became a specialty of English art during the reign of Henry VIII. A transportable art, the practice long ago of wearing or carrying miniatures was a gesture of intimacy. Women often wore them as bracelets and men kept them in their pockets, attached by a ribbon or chain to the gold cases that framed them. Charles Willson Peale and members of his family are among the country's greatest representatives of the art of miniature. The acquisition of miniature portraits by Peale, as well as by his son Raphaelle and his niece Anna Claypoole Peale, opened up a new area of collecting at Bayou Bend, while complementing the museum's impressive collection representing the Peale artistic dynasty.
EBN

Watercolor on ivory
Frame (oval): 3 1/2 x 2 7/8" (8.9 x 7.3 cm)
Gift of Mr. and Mrs. Isaac C. Kerridge
B.2006.24

43 Self-Portrait with Angelica and Portrait of Rachel

c. 1782–85
Charles Willson Peale (1741–1827)
Philadelphia

Offered to Miss Hogg in 1960, this renowned self-portrait of Charles Willson Peale at his easel painting his wife, Rachel, with playful daughter Angelica at his side, was deemed too expensive by Miss Hogg's advising committee at the Museum of Fine Arts, Houston. According to Rudy Wunderlich of Kennedy Galleries, which represented the painting, Miss Hogg turned the painting down. Wunderlich, as he was departing for the airport to return the painting to New York, received an early morning phone call from Miss Hogg, who said, "Would you do an old lady a great favor and hold that painting for a day or so until I can make up my mind? I simply have not been able to sleep all night, thinking about the picture." By the time Wunderlich reached New York, a telegram from Miss Hogg awaited him, advising that regardless of the committee's advice, she was going to purchase the painting. Her instincts, despite (or because of) the sleepless night, could not have been sharper. This self-portrait by one of the country's greatest artists continues to be one of Bayou Bend's most important masterpieces.
EBN

Oil on canvas
36 1/8 x 27 1/8" (91.8 x 68.9 cm)
Gift of Miss Ima Hogg
B.60.49

44 Sauceboat

1770–72
American China Manufactory (1769–72)
Philadelphia

Miss Hogg assembled a notable group of porcelains produced at William Ellis Tucker's Philadelphia firm in the 1820s and 1830s (cat. 74), yet she never expanded her collecting to encompass other American porcelains. Since 1975, objects produced at other factories have been added, thereby presenting a more complete survey. In 1983 the museum had the opportunity to acquire this rare example from the earliest American factory, established in 1769 by Gousse Bonnin and George Anthony Morris in Philadelphia, one of fewer than twenty examples known. In the study of American ceramics, this sauceboat maintains a special place, for it is credited with revising our understanding of this historic venture. In 1947 Arthur Clement recorded it in *Our Pioneer Potters*. At that time, it was assumed the American China Manufactory factory produced earthenware. However, Mrs. George K. Stout, who then owned the sauceboat, believed it was porcelain because the body is translucent. Although Clement had published it, he had not actually examined the piece. Once he had the opportunity to do so, he confirmed Mrs. Stout's assertion, thereby totally revising our understanding of the significance of the American China Manufactory. In February 1951, *Antiques* published this discovery in the article, "Found Bonnin and Morris Porcelain."

Soft-paste porcelain
2 1/4 x 2 5/8 x 4 7/8" (5.7 x 6.7 x 12.4 cm)
Gift of the Friends of Bayou Bend
B.83.4

45 *Tea Table*

1755–90
Newport

In January 1930, only weeks after the historic stock market crash, one of the most substantial collections of American antiques, that formed by the late Philip Flayderman, came to auction at the American Art Association–Anderson Galleries in New York. "Bondome," reviewing the sale in *Antiques*, commented, "Everybody knew that the tea table made by John Goddard for Jabez Bowen would create a sensation: but few, if any, expected that the desire for its possession would create so intense a rivalry as to fetch a closing bid of $29,000." Ever since, these graceful tables have been highly prized by collectors. In 1957, Miss Hogg purchased this one privately. Today, eight are known. While evenly divided between public and private collections, they are no longer within the means of most institutions—the last example realizing more than $8 million at auction in 2005.

Mahogany; no secondary woods intact
26 7/8 x 33 3/4 x 20 1/2" (68.3 x 85.7 x 52.1 cm)
Gift of Miss Ima Hogg
B.57.1

46 Desk-and-Bookcase

1755–1800
Newport

Ima Hogg's correspondence reveals her appreciation of how an object's provenance contributes to one's understanding and interpretation of a piece. In 1952, she purchased from dealer John Walton this iconic Newport desk-and-bookcase. Walton was often forthcoming with information about where he had acquired a piece, but in this instance he was less helpful. Miss Hogg wrote to him, "Though I am pleased to have purchased the beautiful block front secretary with shells, I am very disappointed not to have its pedigree or something of its previous ownership. . . . I would be willing to hold the name of the former owners in confidence . . . but would greatly appreciate being able to have the secretary recorded with as much history as possible for my files. All my pieces of furniture of any value go to a museum. I may add that a fine piece like this secretary deserves to be identified better, don't you think?" Years later the reason for Walton's reticence became evident. The desk had been found in Britain and purchased for Winterthur, only to have Mr. du Pont turn it down. It was then brokered through Walton and Israel Sack.

Mahogany, brass; cedrela odorata,
chestnut, eastern white pine, poplar,
red cedar, soft maple, and white oak
99 3/4 x 44 1/4 x 26 1/4 "
(253.4 x 112.4 x 66.7 cm)
Gift of Miss Ima Hogg
B.69.22

47 Portrait of John Vaughan

c. 1795
Gilbert Stuart (1755–1828)
Philadelphia

Miss Hogg acquired this dashing portrait of John Vaughan as a superb example of the spontaneous brushwork, luminosity, and rich color in the best paintings by Gilbert Stuart, George Washington's image-maker and the major portraitist of post-Revolutionary America. Extensive correspondence between Miss Hogg, the art dealer from whom she acquired the painting, and scholars such as Julian Boyd, the editor of the papers of Thomas Jefferson, shows her tenacity in learning more, and in greater detail, about a sitter and the cultural period a particular artwork evokes. In time, she learned that John Vaughan commissioned the celebrated "Vaughan" portrait of Washington, the first of three types painted by Stuart. She also learned that the sitter himself, a Jamaica-born importer of fine wines in Philadelphia, represented Enlightenment ideals through his association with Jefferson and with the American Philosophical Society, whose library he maintained for over forty years, as well as through his general advocacy of good citizenry in his adopted city of Philadelphia. In this role, he would have been Miss Hogg's kindred spirit.
EBN

Oil on canvas
30 1/8 x 25 1/4" (76.5 x 64.1 cm)
Gift of Miss Ima Hogg
B.61.55

Oil on panel
24 1/8 x 19 3/4" (61.3 x 50.2 cm)
Gift of the Theta Charity Antiques Show
B.91.25

48 Portrait of Mrs. John Trumbull

1820–23
John Trumbull (1756–1843),
New York

He was among the most important
cultural figures in American history,
but John Trumbull and his personal
life were the source of contempora-
neous gossip, especially his hurried
marriage in 1800 to a woman whose
beauty he admired but whose hazy
background he both acknowledged
and then dismissed. He warned a
relative in a letter, for example,
"You will not, therefore, expect to
see a modern fine Lady," referring
to his new wife, Sarah Hope Harvey
Trumbull. Rumors of his wife's
instability and alcoholism persisted
among Trumbull's friends, but he
remained devoted to her and painted
her throughout her life at least thirteen times, notably, with potent
symbols of innocence, Christian
piety, and faithfulness. This panel is
a smaller version of a painting of her
as "Innocence," in which she holds a
bleeding dove (Yale University Art
Gallery). Here Trumbull eliminates
the bird, and raises his fifty-year-
old wife's hand, with its elongated,
elegant fingers, to her breast in a
gesture of piety. These enigmatic
paintings suggest a variety of
complex psychologies, none of
which is mutually exclusive: either
as Trumbull envisioned his wife;
wished her to be; wanted others to
see her; or encouraged her to view
herself. The first work by this
seminal artist to enter Bayou Bend's
paintings collection, it brings its
marriage secrets with it.
EBN

 ## 49 Teapot

1785–98
Shop of William Will (1742–1798)
Philadelphia

In 1953, Miss Hogg began to assemble a group of early American pewter, but she never embraced the medium in the same way she did silver, which she began to collect at the same time. Most of her pewter was acquired between 1958 and 1961, with the encouragement of her advisor Charles Montgomery.

William Will was probably the most important American craftsman working in this medium. Henry Francis du Pont admired the quality and versatility of Will's pewter and set out to assemble a collection, one that eventually comprised thirty-eight objects, and demonstrated his range of designs and forms.

In 1961, Thomas D. Williams, a Connecticut dealer who specialized in pewter, offered Miss Hogg a rare, small Will teapot. Citing "a heavy drain" on her acquisitions budget, she declined. Perhaps she had difficulty reconciling the price; a few months earlier she had acquired from Israel Sack a mid-eighteenth-century silver teapot by Joseph Richardson, Sr., Will's contemporary, for approximately the same price. Two months later, Williams wrote Miss Hogg again, this time to bring to her attention this Will teapot—as it turns out, Mr. du Pont had acquired the example he offered earlier and traded this one in.

Pewter, unidentified wood
7 5/16 x 5 x 8 3/4" (18.6 x 12.7 x 22.2 cm)
Gift of Miss Ima Hogg
B.61.27

ℬℬ 50 Cupboard or Dresser

1800–30
Berks County, Pennsylvania

By contrast to the great mahogany monuments that predominate at Bayou Bend, this boldly proportioned and exuberantly decorated cupboard vies for recognition. Rather than a reflection of the elite, urbane Anglo-American society, this colorful cupboard is an expression of a prosperous, rural German-American culture. These imposing objects were among the principal furniture forms associated with the industrious Germans who came to settle the rural countryside outside Philadelphia. Today this great cupboard, evocative of a people distinguished by its own traditions and possessions, also serves as a reminder that America has always been a melting pot of cultures.

Paint, brass, glass; yellow-poplar
83 1/2 x 63 x 17 7/8"
(212.1 x 160 x 45.4 cm)
Gift of the Theta Charity Antiques Show and the Friends of Bayou Bend
B.79.287

51 Writing-arm Chair

1770–1803
Ebenezer Tracy (1744–1803)
Lisbon, Connecticut

In 1922, Will Hogg purchased "1 Old Writing Arm Windsor" from "I. Sack," at 85 Charles Street, Boston, thus beginning a close collaboration with Bayou Bend that would span seven decades. Ebenezer Tracy's furniture, distinguished by its fine craftsmanship and measured proportions, make him the undisputed patriarch of Windsor chair-making in New England. Bayou Bend's chair has come down in remarkable condition; having escaped refinishing, it retains an early painted surface, and its writing arm reveals a sequence of tack holes. For an explanation of the latter, one need look no further than the museum's portrait by Ralph Earl, which pictures his patron, Dr. Mason Fitch Cogswell, posed in a similarly configured chair (cat. 52). Earl's depictions of the Connecticut well-to-do are not only charming likenesses but invaluable records of contemporary interiors and possessions. His portrait of Cogswell is so precisely rendered that even the medical books in the background can be identified. Two hundred years later, conservator Steve Pine and textile specialist Florine Carr, relying in part on Earl's detailed composition, located wool fibers under some of the remaining tacks which in turn enabled them to re-create the appearance of the chair's original baize cover.

Paint, brass; butternut, chestnut,
Eastern white pine, soft maple,
white oak, yellow-poplar
46 3/4 x 37 x 30" (118.7 x 94 x 76.2 cm)
Gift of Miss Ima Hogg
B.69.409

52 Portrait of Dr. Mason Fitch Cogswell

1791
Ralph Earl (1751–1801)
Hartford

The story behind this animated and engaging portrait of Dr. Mason Fitch Cogswell is poignant and, fittingly, symbolizes loyalty and friendship on two different levels. Dr. Cogswell, the jovial Hartford physician who is the subject of the portrait, arranged the release from debtor's prison of Ralph Earl, a talented artist troubled by debts and hard drinking. Through Cogswell's family connections in Connecticut, he provided the artist with numerous patrons—his own family, his patients, and his friends. In part because of Cogswell's loyalty and support, Earl would go on to become one of the greatest portraitists of the New Republic. Bayou Bend was offered this masterwork in July 1975, but Miss Hogg died unexpectedly one month later in London, before the painting could be sent to Houston on approval. Friends of Miss Hogg provided the funds to acquire the portrait in her honor—a gesture of friendship, support, and loyalty, echoed in the circumstances of the painting itself.
EBN

Oil on canvas
37 1/4 x 32" (94.6 x 81.3 cm)
Museum purchase with funds provided in memory of Miss Ima Hogg, by her friends
B.76.184

THE DINING ROOM, 1780–1810

53 Side Chair, one of a pair

1800
Shop of John Townsend (1732/33–1809)
Newport

New discoveries can prove exhilarating, insightful, and challenging. When this graceful, Neoclassical side chair, and its three mates, were discovered in the mid-1960s, it caused a stir in the antiques world. Pasted inside the rear seat rail was a label for John Townsend, the most renowned of the Newport cabinetmakers, but was it genuine? No one actually knew what his chairs looked like, since no documented example was known. Were it not for the precious label, the chair would be assigned to New York; after all, it corresponds closely to designs and construction details peculiar to that furniture center. With considerable difference in value between a Townsend chair and a generic New York example, many dealers and collectors kept their distance—those who believed in them took a chance and were proven right.

Mahogany; birch, eastern white pine, poplar, soft maple
38 1/2 x 21 3/8 x 21" (97.8 x 54.3 x 53.3 cm)
Gift of Miss Ima Hogg
B.66.11.1

ℬℬ

54 Tumbler

c. 1788
Attributed to John Frederick Amelung's
New Bremen Glass Manufactory, 1784–95
Frederick County, Maryland

The Corning Museum of Glass celebrated the American Bicentennial in 1976 with a book devoted to the New Bremen Glass Manufactory, the largest and most sophisticated glassworks established in eighteenth-century America. This glasshouse, established by John Frederick Amelung in 1784, is notable for the size of the investment, the scale of the manufactory, and the sophistication of the table glass produced there. The Corning Museum book presents an incomparable model for research in American decorative arts; it includes the results of an archaeological excavation and the findings of a nondestructive chemical analysis of archaeological fragments, as well as signed and related glasses, undertaken by the Winterthur Museum analytical laboratory. A year after the publication was released, this tumbler was discovered at an antiques fair in New Jersey. Inscribed "Federal," there can be little question that it commemorates the ratification of the Constitution in 1788. The attribution of the "Federal" tumbler benefited from the findings of the Corning study, and was further substantiated by comparison of its motto to the "Amelung alphabet" devised from other engraved glasses for the Corning study.

Nonlead glass
6 1/8 x 4 9/16 (15.6 x 11.6 cm)
Gift of Houston Junior Woman's Club
B.99.20

BB

55 *Pair of Card Tables*

1795–1810
Charleston

The following experience is hardly
unique: a major study is published
and even before the print is dry,
previously unknown objects surface
that further the understanding and
interpretation of the subject. Such
was the case in 2003, when this
refined pair of Neoclassical card
tables came on the market. Their
discovery was within months of the
publication of *The Furniture of Charleston,
1680–1820*, a three-volume treatise
by Bradford Rauschenberg and John
Bivins, Jr. It is the most comprehensive study to date on any regional
school of American furniture. This
singular pair of tables, though allied
to other Charleston examples, is distinguished by its tops with their
wedge-shaped, radiating panels reminiscent of a Neoclassical architectural fanlight, and by its imported
satinwood veneers, a cabinet wood
much more expensive than
mahogany and therefore rarely
encountered in American furniture.

Satinwood, unidentified inlay; birch,
eastern white pine
Each table, closed: 29 1/2 x 36 1/4 x 16 5/8"
(74.9 x 92.1 x 42.2 cm)
Each table, open: 29 1/2 x 36 1/4 x 33 1/8"
(74.9 x 92.1 x 84.1 cm)
Promised gift of a member of the
W. H. Keenan Family with additional funds
provided by the W. H. Keenan Family
Endowment Fund
B.2004.1.1, .2

BB

56 *Armchair*

1785–1815
Philadelphia

When a masterpiece comes up for auction, it typically generates a great deal of excitement that translates into a great price. In 1991, this armchair and three others, from a suite that probably comprised eight examples in all, were offered by Christie's. According to tradition, the furniture was commissioned by Robert Morris, the fabulously wealthy Philadelphia merchant who signed the Declaration of Independence and who has often been credited as the financier of the American Revolution. Two factors worked in the museum's favor. First, all four chairs were offered at the same sale, rather than individually. Second, their fragile composition, gilded, and painted surfaces would require extensive conservation treatment and financial commitment. These factors may explain the auction's outcome, with the chairs selling below estimate and destined for three public collections—Colonial Williamsburg, Yale University Art Gallery, and Bayou Bend.

Paint, gold leaf; ash, composition, original upholstery foundation
36 1/2 x 20 3/4 x 20 7/8"
(92.7 x 52.7 x 53 cm)
Gift of the Theta Charity Antiques Show
B.91.51

93

THE FEDERAL PARLOR, 1780–1810

57 A Display of the United States

1791
Amos Doolittle (1754–1832)
New Haven, Connecticut

Amos Doolittle's *A Display of the United States of America* was his most ambitious work to date and is recognized as one of the largest prints executed by an eighteenth-century American engraver. It was first issued in 1788 or 1789, coinciding with George Washington's election as president. The image of Washington is surrounded by a heraldic ring representing the states, thus symbolizing their newfound national unity. In Doolittle's original composition, Washington was attired in a suit, suggesting his civilian role as president; however, the artist changed his mind and subsequently depicted him in his general's uniform. What appears to be an aura around the figure of the president is actually where part of the earlier image was erased. As more states joined the union, Doolittle's patriotic composition became more complex, so that over the subsequent years it went through six revisions.

Engraving
22 1/2 x 19" (57.2 x 48.3 cm)
Museum purchase with funds provided by Robert G. Phillips and El Paso Energy in honor of Bill Wise at "One Great Night in November, 2001"
B.2001.29

58 Stand

1784–85
China

This porcelain stand incorporates the emblems of the Society of the Cincinnati, the hereditary organization formed by the American and French officers who served together during the American Revolution. George Washington, like so many of its members, desired Chinese export porcelain bearing the Society's symbols. In August 1786, he purchased an extensive set of 302 pieces consisting of breakfast, tea, and table services. Today it is heralded as the most famous and widely collected of Washington's china. The porcelain's subsequent history is equally interesting. Martha Washington bequeathed the service to her grandson, George Washington Parke Custis, whose collection of Washington artifacts was installed at Arlington House, just across the Potomac from the capital. His home and collection were subsequently inherited by his daughter, Mary, and her husband, General Robert E. Lee. With the advent of the Civil War, the Lees, siding with the Confederacy, fled Arlington, leaving their property to be confiscated by the federal government. Decades later, President William McKinley returned Washington's Cincinnati service to the Lee family.

Hard-paste porcelain
7/16 x 7 11/16 x 5 3/4" (1.2 x 19.5 x 14.6 cm)
Gift of the Jameson family, in honor of
Mr. and Mrs. Robert D. Jameson
B.98.35

59 Side Chair, one of a pair

1785–99
Boston or Salem, Massachusetts

60 Gentleman's Secretary

1790–1820
Salem, Massachusetts

This superb chair was made for Elias Hasket Derby (1739–1799), the first American millionaire. Son of the successful Salem merchant Richard Derby, he not only inherited his father's business acumen, but also his passion for surrounding himself with fine possessions—both generations patronized Paul Revere. The ultimate conspicuous consumer, he commissioned a succession of mansions; each was larger and grander than its predecessor, with the fourth and final one based on designs prepared by the talented young architect Charles Bulfinch. There, along with Revere's glistening silver, the interiors were punctuated with pieces that are among the most sophisticated expressions of Neoclassicism in New England furniture—and, as with any of Derby's possessions, highly prized among collectors today.

China closets and display cabinets were nonexistent in the eighteenth century, so collectors such as Miss Hogg and Henry Francis du Pont adapted their gentleman's secretaries to display the early ceramics, glass, and other objects they acquired. This singular form, expanded beyond the confines of its eighteenth-century predecessors, is virtually exclusive to Salem, although the design, like so much American furniture, is based on British examples. Thomas Sheraton published a design for one, and in his accompanying text explained: "[It] is intended for standing to write at, and therefore the height is adjusted for this purpose...." He goes on to advise that the left cupboard is intended for the business man's ledgers and papers, whereas the one on the right can house his slippers and chamber pot.

Mahogany, ebony; ash, eastern white pine, soft maple
38 x 21 3/4 x 20 5/8" (96.5 x 55.2 x 52.4 cm)
Gift of Miss Ima Hogg
B.61.92.1

Mahogany, eastern white pine, soft maple, unidentified inlay; birch, eastern white pine, yellow-poplar
96 3/8 x 72 1/8 x 20 1/4"
(244.8 x 183.2 x 51.4 cm)
Gift of Miss Ima Hogg
B.61.94

61 Sampler

1798
Polly Snow, b. 1788
Attributed to the School of Ann Waters
Probably Newbury, Massachusetts

Textiles have largely been the province of women collectors, dealers, and scholars. Ima Hogg is an exception to this axiom, and as a result, the collection at Bayou Bend lacks dimension in this medium. This is not indicative of a lack of interest on her part, but of her concern over the responsibility of caring for antique textiles—an uneasiness that can also be perceived in the collection of Southwest Indian art she assembled, which does not include any weavings. Karen and Jim Marrow were surprised to discover that Bayou Bend lacked such a pivotal form as a sampler, an object central to interpreting the position and education of young women in America. They generously offered to seek out and acquire one for the collection.

Silk on linen
15 3/8 x 12 1/2" (39.1 x 31.8 cm)
Gift of Mr. and Mrs. James Marrow
B.98.16

62 Tambour Desk

1794–1810
Attributed to the shop of John (1738–1818) and Thomas (1771–1848) Seymour, partnership 1794–1804, or Thomas Seymour's "Boston Furniture Warehouse" Boston

In January 1930, shortly after the stock market crash and the beginning of the Great Depression, came astounding news that an early American desk was auctioned in New York for $30,000. Ima Hogg must have taken great delight, as any collector would, since the desk, labeled by the cabinetmakers John and Thomas Seymour, was closely related to one in her own collection. Years later, she likely experienced that same excitement all over again when script initials believed to be the Seymours' were discovered on her desk.

Mahogany, unidentified inlay, enameled brass; eastern white pine, red oak
41 3/8 x 37 1/2 x 191/2"
(105.1 x 95.3 x 49.5 cm)
Gift of Miss Ima Hogg
B.65.12

63 Mourning Piece

1807
Ann Vose Bemis (1797–1861)
Boston

This brilliant silk embroidery draws the attention of those passionate about textiles, as well as furniture collectors and scholars. To the latter, the name Vose is a familiar one. Mary Vose (1769–1807), whose daughter Ann fashioned the mourning piece, was the wife of Isaac Vose (1767–1823), a principal in Vose, Son, and Coates, one of Boston's leading cabinet firms. In 1819, following the death of their partner Joshua Coates, Isaac Vose, Sr., and his son contracted with Thomas Seymour (cat. 62) to become their shop foreman. With the talented Seymour engaged, the Vose firm could offer its clientele an expanded repertoire of designs and forms. When Isaac Vose, Sr., died four years later, he had become the most successful Boston cabinetmaker of his day.

Silk taffeta, silk embroidery thread,
applied paper, watercolor, ink,
original reverse-painted glass mat
and gilded frame
17 3/8 x 15 1/2" (44.1 x 39.4 cm) [frame]
Gift of Miss Ima Hogg
B.70.51

ℬℬ

64 Coat of Arms

1785
Hannah Babcock (1769/70–1856)
Boston

In 1961, Miss Hogg received a response from Childs Gallery in Boston to her inquiry about hatchments: "I am sorry to say we do not have any hatchments, and I believe they are fairly scarce and difficult to find." Two decades later, Betty Ring brought this example to the attention of the museum staff which, in addition to its rarity, is insightful for its documentation: "Wrought by H[ann]ah Babcock at Mrs Snow's school, Pemberton Hills, Boston, 1785." Since the time of this acquisition, Mrs. Ring has researched these embroideries and, by doing so, has completely revised our understanding of this textile form. Rather than "hatchments," or coats of arms of deceased persons displayed during a period of mourning, these embroideries were fashioned as prestigious household decorations by young girls at boarding schools as part of their education. They are a textile art form that is wholly unique to New England.

Satin, silk embroidery thread, original frame
33 x 33" (83.8 x 83.8 cm)
Gift of Mr. and Mrs. James Anderson, Jr., Mr. and Mrs. Thomas D. Anderson, Mr. and Mrs. Mark Edwin Andrews, Mr. and Mrs. A. Leslie Ballard, Jr., Mrs. Patricia B. Carter, Mr. and Mrs. B. W. Crain, Mrs. Jean Forsythe Garwood, Morgan Garwood, Susan Garwood, Dr. and Mrs. Mavis P. Kelsey, Mrs. William H. Lane, Mr. and Mrs. Maurice McAshan, Mr. and Mrs. Albert Maverick III, Mr. Hugo Neuhaus, and Mr. Herbert C. Wells
B.84.7

65 Mourning Piece

c. 1815–18
Attributed to Almira Earle
(1800–1831)
Painting attributed to John Johnston
(1753–1818)
Milton, Massachusetts

Betty Ring, a scholar of American
needlework and material culture, has
enjoyed a long affiliation with Bayou
Bend as a docent, a member of the
Bayou Bend Committee, and a
friend of Miss Hogg's. She tells of
her 1966 visit to Elizabeth Daniel's
shop, Gooseneck Antiques in Chapel
Hill, North Carolina, where she
admired an exquisite group of
embroidered pictures, including this
remarkable example, but was told
they were not for sale. She returned
to Houston and mentioned the visit
to Miss Hogg, who later visited Mrs.
Daniel herself. The Daniels were
captivated by their guest. Before
leaving, Miss Hogg purchased three
of the embroideries, including this
spectacular composition that George
Daniel had given his wife as an
anniversary gift.

Silk taffeta, silk and silk chenille embroidery
threads, watercolor, reverse-painted mat
34 1/4 x 33" (87 x 83.8 cm) [frame]
Gift of Miss Ima Hogg
B.70.52

66 *Pleasure Party by a Mill*

Late 1780s
James Peale (1749–1831)
Bloomsbury, New Jersey

Oil on canvas
26 1/4 x 40 1/8" (66.7 x 101.9 cm)
Gift of Miss Ima Hogg
B.62.16

Miss Hogg acquired this major landscape painting in 1962 as a work by Charles Willson Peale, one of the most celebrated painters of his day, as well as an inventor, scientist, public museum founder, and the patriarch of the country's first family dynasty of artists. Since about 1964, however, the painting has been reassigned to his younger brother James on the basis of a related sketch-book. Correspondence indicates that Miss Hogg may not have been initially pleased about the reassigned attribution, for at the time, the superb skills of James Peale were still little known. As she wrote in a letter to a Peale descendant in 1965,

"Of course this was a great disappointment because we had been seeking an early landscape and it made it more important to have a Charles Willson Peale." Nonetheless, she added, "We like the painting very much and feel it is an excellent example of early American landscape painting." Miss Hogg was right; the painting is a superb example of early American landscape painting in the decades preceding the rise of the Hudson River School, and helped to raise public and critical estimation of James Peale's artistic career. EBN

67 Landscape Looking Toward Sellers Hall from Mill Bank

c. 1818
Charles Willson Peale (1741–1827)
Philadelphia

Oil on canvas
15 x 21 1/4" (38.1 x 54 cm)
Gift of Mrs. James W. Glanville
B.98.12

With this generous gift from Nancy Hart Glanville, Bayou Bend at last secured the Charles Willson Peale landscape Miss Hogg had always wanted for the collection (see cat. 66). Peale's interlude as a landscape painter came late in his career, when he retired to the life of a gentleman-farmer at Belfield, his home outside Philadelphia and the locus of his landscape experiments in horticulture and in painting. This painting is one of two Peale painted for his favorite son-in-law, Coleman Sellers, whose ancestral home is pictured in the distance. The other painting that forms the pendant is from Sellers Hall looking towards Mill Bank, joining together two vistas among a cluster of family properties owned by Sellers and his relatives in a charming, balanced composition radiant with summer sunlight. This small but vibrant painting enriches Bayou Bend's presentation of landscape as it became invested with scientific, spiritual, and national significance over the course of the nineteenth century.

EBN

68 Still Life with Vegetables

1826
James Peale (1749–1831)
Philadelphia

Oil on canvas
20 x 26 1/2" (50.8 x 67.3 cm)
Gift of the Theta Charity Antiques Show
in honor of Mrs. Fred T. Couper, Jr.
B.85.2

Reflective of the American art market in the eighteenth and early nineteenth centuries, Bayou Bend's paintings collection contains mostly portraits. This acquisition in 1985 added a new genre of painting to the collection, still life, which the Peale family established and popularized in the early 1800s. At age seventy-six, his failing eyesight (but certainly not diminishing skill) prompted James Peale to cede his work in miniature painting to his daughters. He began painting expansive still lifes such as this one, which bursts forth with fresh, crisply rendered and brightly colored garden vegetables bathed in a soothing, golden light. Possibly exhibited in the Pennsylvania Academy of Fine Arts exhibition of 1827, this still life is signed by the artist and inscribed to his daughter Anna Claypoole Peale Staughton, and was copied by the artist two years later in a version now owned by Winterthur.
EBN

BB

69 *Pair of Side Chairs*

1808
Designed by Benjamin Henry Latrobe (1764–1820)
Painted decoration attributed to George Bridport
(1783–1819)
Baltimore or Philadelphia

In 1963, Berry B. Tracy organized the landmark exhibition *Classical America 1815–1845* at the Newark Museum, highlighting a chair from the same suite as the pair at Bayou Bend to grace the catalogue cover. That chair was lent by the Philadelphia Museum of Art, which had received it as a gift almost thirty years earlier, and at the time of the Newark show, its history had yet to be unearthed. In the intervening years, additional pieces from the suite emerged from different branches of the family in which it had descended. With some genealogical sleuthing, Beatrice Garvan, a curator at the museum, was able to reconstruct the chairs' provenance, but more importantly, to identify them as part of the commission that Benjamin Henry Latrobe, the

brilliant architect who was the nation's leading proponent of Grecian design, completed for William Waln in 1808. Placing them among the earliest of the American manifestations of the style, the chairs must have been quite grand in the Waln drawing room.

Paint, gold leaf, cane; maple, yellow-poplar, composition
Each: 34 1/2 x 20 x 20 1/2"
(87.6 x 50.8 x 52.1 cm)
Museum purchase with funds provided by the Agnes Cullen Arnold Endowment Fund
B.90.9.1–.2

ℬℬ

70 *Sofa*

1810–30
New York

This sofa, with its graceful, undulating dolphin supports, belongs to a group of related New York examples. Although the dolphin is a popular classical motif referring to Venus, its use here may have been partly inspired by a contemporary design for "Nelson's Chairs" that Thomas Sheraton published in 1806. The latter paid homage to Admiral Horatio Nelson following his defeat of the French, and his own death at Trafalgar a year earlier. These imaginative New York adaptations became more widely known in the early 1960s when Jacqueline Kennedy introduced one of these sofas into the Red Room during her restoration of the White House interiors. Assured that collectors of American art would be supportive of her plans, the First Lady invited Henry Francis du Pont to chair her fine arts committee and Miss Hogg to be a member.

Mahogany; ash, cherry, eastern white pine, mahogany
34 3/4 x 94 1/4 x 27" (88.3 x 239.4 x 68.6 cm)
Gift of the Theta Charity Antiques Show
B.78.79

71 Soup Tureen

1817
Manufactory of Andrew Ellicott Warner
(1786–1870)
Baltimore

Inscribed in Latin, "Renowned for his valor, beloved for his virtues," this grand tureen was part of an impressive silver service presented to Commodore Stephen Decatur, Jr., the brilliant naval hero, by the citizens of Baltimore in 1817. Two decades later, his widow, then virtually destitute, was forced to sell their silver, and Bayou Bend's tureen may have been among a group of objects which were vended in New York in 1840. Although other pieces of the service were known, the soup tureen did not surface until 1979, and it was acquired for Bayou Bend the following year. The significance of the accession is underscored by its extensive publication record in the twenty-five years since it was added to the collection, appearing in three exhibitions and their accompanying catalogues, two books, and five articles in *Antiques* magazine.

Silver
12 1/2 x 14 3/4 x 9 1/2"
(31.8 x 37.5 x 24.1 cm)
Gift of the Theta Charity Antiques Show
in honor of Betty Black Hatchett
B.80.6

A VIEW of the BOMBARDMENT of Fort McHenry, near Baltimore, by the British fleet. taken from the Observatory, under the Command of Admirals Cochrane & Cockburn, on the morning of the 13th of Sep.r 1814 which lasted 24 hours, & thrown from 1500 to 1800 shells in the Night attempted to land by forcing a passage up the ferry branch but were repulsed with great loss.

References.
A. Fort McHenry.
B. Lazaretto.
C. Salisance House.
Admiral Ship. North Point.
E. Ferry and Fort.

BB

72 *A View of the Bombardment of Fort McHenry*

c. 1815
John Bower (active 1809–19)
Philadelphia

Aquatint
12 5/8 x 17 5/8" (32.1 x 44.8 cm)
Museum purchase with funds provided by
"One Great Night in November, 1990"
B.90.14

A major addition to the museum's small collection of prints is John Bower's stirring *A View of the Bombardment of Fort McHenry*—the only contemporary depiction of the Battle of Baltimore. Today this engagement is best remembered as the inspiration for Francis Scott Key, who at the time was aboard a prisoner-of-war ship in the harbor, to immortalize the Americans' valiant defense in a poem. Key's verse eventually became the lyrics for our national anthem, "The Star Spangled Banner." While Bower's artistic abilities were not nearly as adroit as his timing, the museum's print, one of only eight known examples, is an enduring American image.

73 Center Table

1820–40
New York

From the time Miss Hogg acquired this unique table for the Chillman Suite, it was admired for its beautifully rendered landscape. However, over the years, the composition lost much of its definition as its varnished surface yellowed. Thirty years later, in an unusual partnership between paintings and furniture conservators, Jill Whitten and Rob Proctor collaborated with Steve Pine to study, clean, and conserve the finish. Their examination determined the varnish was not original, and identified there had been an earlier restoration campaign. In turn, these findings championed the proposal to remove the degraded finish. As the varnish was carefully removed, and the craquelure cleaned, it was hoped an artist's signature would emerge. One did not, but a glorious landscape did!

Paint, gold leaf, mahogany; cherry, eastern white pine, mahogany
27 1/2 x 36" (69.9 x 91.4 cm)
Gift of Miss Ima Hogg
B.69.526

THE CHILLMAN PARLOR, 1810–40

74 *Pair of Vases*

1827–38
William Ellis Tucker (1800–1832),
Tucker and Hulme, Tucker and Hemphill,
or Joseph Hemphill (active 1826–38)
Philadelphia

One never knows when a great object might surface. In 1972, Bayou Bend's assistant curator, Dean Failey, was on a research trip to learn more about an early landscape in the collection (cat. 66). At the library of the American Philosophical Society in Philadelphia, he studied James Peale's only known sketchbook. There he discovered a group of drawings that confirmed the reattribution of the work to James, the younger brother of Charles Willson Peale, and helped identify the location as the Musconetcong Creek near Bloomsbury, New Jersey. When Failey visited the site, whom should he encounter but James Ogelsby Peale, the artist's great-great-great-grandson. Striking up a conversation, Mr. Peale happened to mention he owned a pair of Tucker vases that once belonged to his artistic ancestor. Failey's curatorial curiosity aroused, he asked if he might see them, and subsequently, if they might be for sale. Mr. Peale agreed—taking great pleasure in knowing that they would be exhibited near his ancestor's landscape, which was painted not far from his own home.

Porcelain
11 1/2 x 5 5/8 x 5 1/4" (29.2 x 14.3 x 13.3 cm)
Gift of Miss Ima Hogg
B.72.118. 1,.2

75 Vase

1832
Shop of John Ewan (1786–1852)
Charleston

No other object in the Bayou Bend Collection has come down with such extensive documentation as the classically inspired vase presented to the Reverend Samuel Gilman in 1832. Commissioned from John Ewan by a group of Charlestonians, it honored the author of "The National Ode," a poem Gilman had penned urging national unity. This was a time of dissention, as South Carolina declared the Federal government's tariff laws null and void. Once the vase was completed, the silversmith advertised it would be on display in his shop "for the inspection of the subscribers and other[s]." At the time it was conferred, a letter of presentation was published by the *Charleston Courier*, and the original letter accompanied the vase and has remained with it. The urn was highly prized by Gilman and his family, as attested by these words from his widow, Caroline: "Millions could not buy the vase."

Silver
13 x 9" (diam.) (33 x 22.9 cm)
Gift of William James Hill and
Miss Ima Hogg, by exchange
B.88.19

BB

76 Pitcher

1815
Manufactory of Thomas Fletcher (1787–1866)
and Sidney Gardiner (1785–1827),
partnership 1808–c. 1830
Boston and Philadelphia

In 1977, Evelyn Houstoun gave this
boldly executed silver pitcher she had
acquired from a distant cousin of
her late husband. Commissioned for
an ancestor of his, it was a fitting gift
with which to honor him. The vessel
introduced the silver of Thomas
Fletcher and Sidney Gardiner, the
preeminent American silversmiths
working in the second and third
decades of the nineteenth century.
Once the piece entered the collection, staff and docents began to
research its history. A genealogy
divulged the existence of its original
bill of sale dated 1815—but where
was that document now? Family
members were contacted; however,
initial efforts proved futile. Then,
a few years later, a letter arrived
from a descendent with a copy of
the bill that clearly describes this
monumental vessel: "1 Silver Pitcher,
round on Square Pedistal & claw feet
/ chased leaves on the body & lid,
with dolphin Top $150.00," an
astounding sum for that time.

Silver
13 1/2 x 6 1/2 x 10 1/8"
(34.3 x 16.5 x 25.7 cm)
Gift of Mrs. James P. Houstoun, Jr.,
in memory of Mr. James P. Houstoun, Jr.
B.77.16

77 Ariadne

1835
Asher Brown Durand (1796–1886),
after John Vanderlyn (1775–1852),
New York

John Vanderlyn's painting of Ariadne received wide acclaim when it was exhibited in Paris; however, in America, it became the subject of controversy and was condemned for its nudity. The response in this country thwarted Vanderlyn's efforts to place it with a patron and, eventually, he sold the painting to his friend and fellow artist Asher B. Durand, whose ambition was to reproduce it as a print. In the 1830s, Durand's abilities as an engraver were unequaled, and many consider that his print of Ariadne surpasses the original oil. However, like Vanderlyn, Durand soon discovered there was limited interest in the composition. The museum's version is a proof impression, that is, a working copy which the engraver would have approved before the title was added and it was released for public sale. As such, it possesses a greater significance and rarity. Furthermore, it bears an intriguing pencil inscription, "Ariadne—gift of J. F. Weir." John Ferguson Weir was an artist and friend of Durand, which raises the possibility that he acquired it directly from the engraver.

Line engraving
17 x 20 1/4" (43.2 x 51.4 cm)
Gift of the Bayou Bend Docent Organization
B.95.2

78 Solar Lamp

1843–51
Cornelius & Co. (active 1839–51)
Philadelphia

In 1783, the year that witnessed the signing of the peace treaty that ended the American Revolution, another revolution, one in lighting, was just beginning. It is hard to imagine today, but up to that time, there had been no significant improvements in lighting since antiquity. In the late 1960s, Miss Hogg and curator David Warren strove to suggest the momentous impact of this innovation in the Chillman Suite. Argand and sinumbra lamps were introduced, but the third major type of lighting device, the solar lamp, was not represented. In 1843, Robert Cornelius received a United States patent for a lard lamp that employed an Argand burner. It burned inexpensive fuel so brightly and efficiently that it inspired its name—"solar." The museum's lamp is magnificently conceived and executed. Its cut-glass column was hollowed out and filled with mercury, which was probably intended to fascinate more so than to reflect.

Glass, brass, iron, marble, and mercury
31 1/4 x 9 1/4 x 9 1/4" (79.4 x 23.5 x 23.5 cm)
Museum purchase with funds provided by the Jack R. McGregor Endowment Fund and the Museum Collectors
B.2004.3

BB

79 *Portrait of James Cornell Biddle*

1841
Thomas Sully (1783–1872)
Philadelphia

Miss Hogg considered her collection not as a memorial to herself but as a living and changing body of artwork, parts of which could be exchanged if it would improve the collection as a whole. This occurred in 1981, when Bayou Bend acquired this dashing portrait of a Philadelphia lawyer, James Cornell Biddle, by Thomas Sully, the most famous portraitist of his day. The acquisition was made by selling lesser works in the collection and combining funds with those generously contributed by the Friends of Bayou Bend. Miss Hogg thus ensured that supreme quality would be the motivating factor behind any Bayou Bend acquisition, including this prime example of Sully's renowned ability to create an atmosphere of relaxed elegance for his sitters. As one American art critic phrased it during the Civil War era: "One always feels at least in good society among [Sully's] portraits."
EBN

Oil on canvas
36 1/4 x 28 1/8" (92.1 x 71.4 cm)
Gift of Miss Ima Hogg and Hirschl and Adler Galleries, by exchange, with an additional gift from the Friends of Bayou Bend
B.81.11

80 Compote

1830–45
Massachusetts

Miss Hogg began to acquire early American glass in the 1920s, probably spurred on more by the idea of using it as decoration than to methodically form an encyclopedic collection. She was particularly attracted to colorful "Stiegel" pocket bottles, vessels produced by window and bottle glass factories, and pressed pictorial flasks. By contrast, her response to pressed "Sandwich" glass was temperate, as evidenced by the presence of only two examples in her collection—this outstanding compote and a relatively common salt dish. Examples such as the compote have long been admired as masterworks of their genre, their manufacture indicative of the principal contribution Americans made in the history of glassmaking, machine pressing.

Lead glass
6 3/8 x 10 1/2 x 8 3/4"
(16.2 x 26.7 x 22.2 cm)
Gift of Miss Ima Hogg
B.70.8

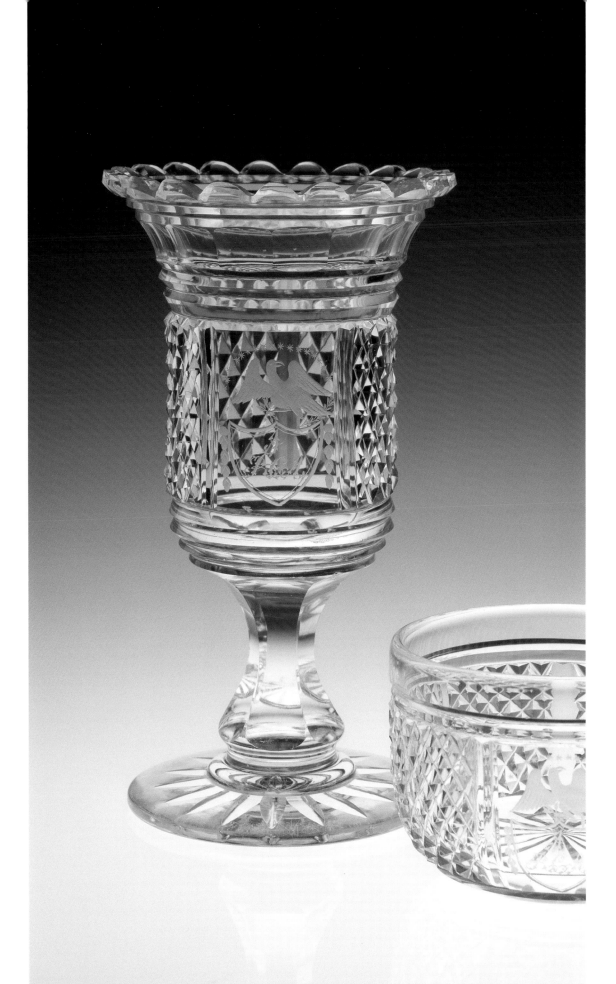

ꓭꓭ

81 Celery Glass

1812–27
Attributed to Bakewell, Page, and Bakewell, 1813–27, or
Boston Glass Manufactory, 1812–27
Pittsburgh or South Boston

In the second decade of the nineteenth century, two American glassmakers, Benjamin Bakewell in Pittsburgh and Thomas Cains in South Boston, became the first in the country to produce cut glass. The recent discovery of this elegant celery glass, sporting an American eagle perched on a shield containing the initials of its first owner, raises an intriguing challenge. Which of the two factories produced this rare vessel? Bakewell's manufactory has been well researched, and a large body of work is associated with it. Included among these is a pair of decanters with similar decoration that were made for President James Madison. By comparison, little is known of Cains's production, and not a single object can be ascribed to the enterprise. While it is tempting to attribute this masterpiece of American glass to the former, it has a history of ownership in New England that offers the tantalizing possibility of its being the first piece of cut glass attributed to Thomas Cains. The key to unraveling this mystery probably lies in the identification of the engraved initials, which has so far proved elusive.

Lead glass
9 3/4 x 5 1/2" (24.8 x 14 cm)
Museum purchase with funds provided by the Marian and Speros Martel Early Americana Accessions Endowment Fund, honoring William S. Kilroy, Sr.
B.2006.7

82 Eagle

1860–90
Attributed to Wilhelm Schimmel (1817–1890)
Cumberland County, Pennsylvania

A number of Miss Hogg's collector friends were attracted to the objects that have long been categorized as "folk art." Henry Francis du Pont and Electra Havemeyer Webb assembled extensive folk art collections at Winterthur and Shelburne, respectively, and Maxim Karolik's assemblage formed the cornerstone of the superb collection at the Museum of Fine Arts, Boston. Edgar and Bernice Chrysler Garbisch bequeathed their works to a number of American institutions, including the Museum of Fine Arts, Houston. Ima Hogg's principal, and brief, foray into folk sculpture was in the mid-1950s when she visited the legendary Edith Gregor Halpert at the Downtown Gallery in New York. Among her handful of purchases there was one of Wilhelm Schimmel's signature eagles. Halpert founded her business in 1926, at a time when few in New York bought and sold avant-garde American art, and none dealt in folk art. She represented a virtual "who's who" of contemporary American artists, including Stuart Davis, Georgia O'Keeffe, and Charles Sheeler. Halpert and others perceived a simple yet direct relationship between folk sculpture and contemporary art, proclaiming these naive objects as the "ancestors" of modern art.

Paint; willow and eastern white pine
12 x 17 x 9" (30.5 x 43.2 x 22.9 cm)
Gift of Miss Ima Hogg
B.57.69

83 Penn's Treaty with the Indians

c. 1830–40
Edward Hicks (1780–1849)
Bucks County, Pennsylvania

Oil on canvas
17 5/8 x 23 5/8" (44.8 x 60 cm)
Gift of Alice C. Simkins in memory
of Alice Nicholson Hanszen
B.77.46

This painting by Edward Hicks was given to
Bayou Bend in 1977 by Alice Simkins, who is a
relative of the Hogg family and a trustee of the
Museum of Fine Arts, Houston. This significant
painting on a patriotic theme may have been a
latecomer to the collection, yet it was among the
first American paintings acquired by the Hogg
family. In 1922, Will Hogg was the successful
bidder on a large collection of Windsor
furniture, as well as this painting, in the

auction of the Jacob Paxson Temple collection
of early American furniture and objects of art
in New York City. At precisely that moment the
Hoggs were beginning to develop and focus their
collecting activities on Americana. Thus it offers
compelling testimony to the strong role played by
Miss Hogg's older brother Will in the formation,
development, and encouragement of Miss Hogg's
life-long dedication to American art.
EBN

THE TEXAS ROOM, 1840–60

84 Pitcher

c. 1848–50
France (body); decoration may have been
executed in the United States

In 1954, Charles Wright, the antiques
and silver buyer for Neiman Marcus
in Dallas, brought this unique pitcher
to Miss Hogg's attention. Executed
with an exacting hand, the vessel
sports a portrait of Zachary Taylor
on one side, the Battle of Buena
Vista on the reverse, and Taylor's
popular appellation, "Rough and
Ready," beneath the spout. Miss
Hogg's response to Wright conveys
her obvious delight with the purchase, Taylor being a historical
figure who interested her because
of his associations with Texas: "I am
enjoying the Zachary Taylor jug and
the Spode mug. I have hung my
large print of the Battle of Buena
Vista over the chest where the jug
stands and the picture on the jug
is identical with that of the print.
It makes it very interesting." The
print she refers to is a chromolithograph of the engagement upon
which the china artist based his
precise rendering.

Hard-paste porcelain
9 5/8 x 6 1/4 x 9" (24.4 x 15.9 x 22.9 cm)
Gift of Miss Ima Hogg
B.54.16

128

85 *Portrait of Margaret Lea Houston (Mrs. Sam Houston)*

c. 1860
Photographer unknown
Possibly Texas

In 1839, Margaret Moffette Lea first met General Sam Houston, then the former president of the Republic of Texas. They were married within the year, and despite her husband's widely known faults, she remained utterly devoted to him through twenty-three years of marriage and eight children. Margaret's daguerreotype possesses a poignancy, as it was taken about the time Texas seceded from the Union, which prompted her husband's removal as governor of Texas, since he had been opposed to the decision. This insightful personal portrait, significant as a historical image, is also pivotal as the first photograph to enter the collection of the Museum of Fine Arts, Houston. The treasured likeness was a gift to Miss Hogg, and therefore predates the establishment of a department of photography in 1976. Under the direction of Anne Wilkes Tucker, the department's founding curator, the museum's photography collection has grown over the past three decades from this single image to an internationally recognized assemblage with more than twenty-two thousand works.

Daguerreotype
Image: 3 5/8 x 2 5/8" (9.2 x 6.7 cm)
Case: 3/4 x 4 3/4 x 3 3/4"
(1.9 x 12.1 x 9.5 cm)
Gift of Miss Ima Hogg
B.89.19

86 Infant Flora

1861
Erastus Dow Palmer (1817–1904)
New York

During the 1950s and 1960s, as Ima
Hogg began to assemble a collection
of portraiture to complement her
decorative arts, she concentrated on
eighteenth-century artists. In fact, at
that time, there was generally less
attention paid to nineteenth-century
art. Since 1975, a concerted effort
has been made to introduce works by
such early nineteenth-century masters as John Trumbull (cat. 48),
Thomas Sully (cat. 79), and
Rembrandt Peale. Complementing
their paintings and adding further
dimension to the collection is the
portrait bust *Infant Flora* by Erastus
Dow Palmer. Subjects such as this
one had immense appeal to the
Victorians, who admired them as
expressions of young innocence.
But tastes change, and a century
later American Classical sculpture
was dismissed as overly sentimental
and, therefore, largely overlooked by
most collectors and curators. By the
1970s, those attitudes and prejudices
began to diminish as nineteenth-
century American art was being
rediscovered.

Marble
16 5/8 x 11 5/8 x 7" (42.2 x 29.5 x 17.8 cm)
Gift of William James Hill in honor of
Carroll and Harris Masterson III
B.94.18

87 Gaming Table

1830–45
New York

Individuals and institutions strive to collect ahead of the proverbial pack. These days it has become more and more challenging to identify a group of objects that is out of fashion and has escaped notice by the market-place. This sophisticated rosewood gaming table, with its composition marble top and graceful scrolled supports, embodies the finest quali-ties of the late Grecian furniture popular in the second quarter of the nineteenth century. Conceived and executed in a restrained fashion, the table pays homage to classical design, yet reflects an interpretation that is in marked contrast with the heavily carved, gilded furniture of earlier decades. Perhaps because the design is so understated, the style is one that has yet to be fully appreciated.

Rosewood, marble; eastern white pine
30 1/2 x 21 7/8 x 21 7/8"
(77.5 x 55.6 x 55.6 cm)
Museum purchase with funds provided by the W. H. Keenan Family Endowment Fund
B.2005.7

The leopard with the harmless kid laid down,
And not one savage beast was seen to frown,

The wolf did with the lambkin dwell in peace,
His grim carnivrous nature there did cease;

The lion with the fatling on did move,
A little child was leading them in love;

When the great PENN his famous treaty made
With INDIAN chiefs beneath the elm tree's shade.

88 *Peaceable Kingdom*

c. 1826–28
Edward Hicks (1780–1849)
Bucks County, Pennsylvania

Oil on canvas
32 3/8 x 42 3/8" (82.2 x 107.6 cm)
Gift of Miss Ima Hogg
B.54.1

Few American artists are as beloved as Edward Hicks, a devout Pennsylvania Quaker preacher and painter. Throughout his life, Hicks obsessively painted the subject of the biblical promise of a peaceable kingdom on earth. More than sixty of these paintings are known. Naively and at times crudely painted, Hicks's canvases nonetheless radiate passion and charm. Toylike animals; placid landscape scenes, mostly of the Delaware Water Gap; and renditions of William Penn's Treaty with the Indians consistently populate Hicks's kingdoms—so peaceable in their ideal of universal harmony, yet weighted with national and religious concerns of the time. Bayou Bend's kingdom is one of eight known versions that include rhymes in their borders referring to the biblical prophecy of Isaiah, in which is expressed the hope and promise of peace on earth. Intertwined in rhyme with the Bible is the historical event of William Penn's treaty, believed by Hicks to represent a partial fulfillment of Isaiah's biblical prophecy. Hicks's canvases may appear naive, but their underlying sources and motivations suggest a rare complexity in the field of so-called American "folk art."
EBN

89 Storage Jar

c.1840–50
Thomas Chandler
(active c. 1840–50)
Edgefield District, South Carolina

Miss Hogg possessed a great affinity for ceramics and during her lifetime collected more than 1,500 examples. Her prime interest was focused on British delft, salt-glazed stoneware, agateware, and mottled glazed pieces, objects that for the most part coincide in date with the American colonial period. She also developed a fondness for the porcelains produced in Philadelphia at the Tucker factory, as well as vessels with a Rockingham-type glaze from American manufactories. In the 1970s, she began to acquire American utilitarian stoneware dating from the 1840s through the 1890s, although these purchases were never acquired in the quantity and quality that distinguished the other ceramics she collected. This large storage jar is certainly the finest of this group; it is notable because of its incised signature by one of the most prominent southern potters.

Alkaline-glazed stoneware
19 1/2 x 16 5/8 x 16 1/2"
(49.5 x 42.2 x 41.9 cm)
Gift of Miss Ima Hogg
B.74.27

90 *Churn*

1869–84
H. Wilson & Co. (active 1869–84)
Guadalupe County, Texas

Fourteen pieces of early Texas pottery that Bayou Bend acquired in 2001 were first exhibited at the Museum of Fine Arts, Houston, in *The Wilson Potters: An African-American Enterprise in 19th-Century Texas*. The installation prompted a powerful response from Hiram Butler, one of Houston's principal contemporary art dealers:

The Wilson pots were unlike any I had known in a museum. They were rough and in various shades of brown; presumably, the color of the mud from which they were made. They were vertical in orientation, broader at the top, and had tiny handles unfit for use. Put together in the case, they looked like a group of broad-shouldered, motionless men, perhaps even bound.

As rough hewn as these pots were, there was an elegance about them, a quiet, and a stillness. Three lines from T. S. Eliot's *Four Quartets* sprung to mind:

Can words or music reach
The stillness, as a Chinese jar still
Moves perpetually in its stillness.

And then I remembered some old pots I saw as a child when playing in a barn at my grandmother Standridge's cotton gin. Two disparate images came together in my mind with a shared severity—crude pots in a barn and the most distilled of Modern poetry.

. . .

Had I not seen the Wilson pot exhibition, I would not own a Texas pot and I would not have thought of these objects the way I do. I look at this simple pot every day and it gives me great pleasure.

Hiram Butler
Devin Borden Hiram Butler Gallery

Salt-glazed stoneware
20 x 11" (50.8 x 27.9 cm)
Gift of Houston Junior Woman's Club
B.2001.10

91 *Parlor Set*

1855
Shop of John Henry Belter (1804–1865)
New York

In his book *American Treasure Hunt: The Legacy of Israel Sack*, Harold Sack recalled a story that illustrates Miss Hogg's discernment as a collector:

> I think my fondest memory of Miss Ima is of the day I called on her in Texas when she'd already turned her home at Bayou Bend over to the museum and had moved into an apartment, where she still had a few fine early American pieces.
>
> We were chatting, and then she said, "Harold, I've got something here to show you."
>
> We went into another room where she had a recently acquired piece, a sofa by John Henry Belter, circa 1850. It was part of a new nineteenth-century collection she was assembling. In Bayou Bend, there is now a room, the Belter Parlor, dedicated to the creations of that nineteenth-century craftsman.

> "Well, Harold," she asked, "what do you think of my Belter piece?"
>
> That nineteenth-century style had never been my cup of tea, and while I was polite about her sofa, I must have made it quite clear to Miss Ima I was unimpressed. In her most colloquial fashion, she shook her head sadly, and said, "Harold, there's the future. You'd better get with it!"
>
> And, as she had so often been during her long life, Miss Ima's good judgment and taste, her nerve and her independence would again be absolutely right.

American Treasure Hunt: The Legacy of Israel Sack, Harold Sack with Max Wilk, 1986, p. 183.

Set consists of two sofas, two armchairs, four side chairs, a center table, and étagère
Rosewood, rosewood veneer; ash, black walnut, brass
Gift of the estate of Miss Ima Hogg
B.81.9.1–.10

THE BELTER PARLOR, 1850–70

92 *View of Gloucester, Mass.*

c. 1856
L. H. Bradford & Co.'s Lith. (1854–59),
after Fitz Henry Lane (1804–1865)
Boston

Chromolithograph
21 5/8 x 35 3/4" (54.9 x 90.8 cm)
Museum purchase with funds provided
by Jerry, Marvy, Jon, Walter, Richard, and
Scott Finger in memory of Ronny Finger
at "One Great Night in November, 2000"
B.2000.18

American prints were never acquired in any sizable numbers by Miss Hogg, which is difficult to reconcile, since in the 1920s and 1930s she formed a collection of more than one hundred works on paper by twentieth-century masters. David Warren recalls a conversation in which Miss Hogg related that works on paper were a medium that held a personal appeal, possessing an intimacy that she found so satisfying. Since 1975, there has been a dedicated effort to add important prints and thereby develop a depth more consistent with other media in the collection. Fitz Henry Lane, the preeminent American marine painter, began his career as a lithographer. His *The National Lancers with the Reviewing Officers on Boston Common* of 1837 (also in the Bayou Bend Collection) represents the artist at the beginning of his career, plying his skill as a printmaker, whereas this serene landscape of Gloucester, where he made his home, is based on a painting of his mature period.

93 Sardine Box

1866–67
William Gale, Jr. (1825–1885)
New York

Ima Hogg was motivated to bring
together a group of objects that speak
to our national history and identity.
However, she was attracted to pieces
principally for their aesthetic quali-
ties rather than their historical
associations. Ultimately, the genius
of the Bayou Bend Collection lies
in the diverse approaches it presents
to American material culture. For
example, take this little sardine box
by William Gale, Jr. It is satisfying
for its design and notable for its
rarity, as it is the only silver American
sardine box known. Yet it can be
appreciated in myriad other ways,
as evocative of the social history and
technical achievements of the period.
At one time, sardines, due to their
perishability, would rarely have
been found on the dining table, but
with the invention of canning in
the 1820s, these delicacies could be
preserved and became more widely
available. And, what would be more
fitting to celebrate their introduction
to the dining room table than a
silver casket, elevated by a quartette
of sprightly dolphins and capped
by a silver knop that disclosed the
nature of its choice contents.

Silver
4 1/2 x 5 7/8 x 4 7/8" (11.4 x 15 x 12.4 cm)
Gift of Chris and Tom Alan Cunningham in
honor of Jeanne Moran Cunningham at
"One Great Night in November, 2002"
B.2002.30

BB

94 Soup Tureen

c. 1858
Gorham Manufacturing Company
(active 1831–present)
Providence

As Miss Hogg began collecting
American silver in the 1950s, she
developed an ardent predilection
for earlier objects and primarily
focused on the colonial period.
The collection she formed is entirely
consistent with what most of the
principal institutions and collectors
were acquiring at the time. The
perception of silver, like other
decorative arts media, was that after
1825, design and craftsmanship
suffered a decline, so accordingly
there was little reason to seek out
the later objects. While some
colonial silver has been added to
the collection since 1975, there has
been a concerted effort to introduce
great nineteenth-century examples,
such as this exceptional Gorham
soup tureen that fully embraces the
rich aesthetic of the Rococo Revival
and even prophesies the tenets of
the Aesthetic Movement.

Silver
11 3/4 x 16 1/8 x 10 1/4" (29.8 x 41 x 26 cm)
Gift of Houston Junior Woman's Club
B.95.1

ℬℬ

95 *Pitcher*

1845–60
Samuel Kirk (1793–1872), now
Kirk Stieff Company, est. 1815
Baltimore

Even museums have limited means to store and care for works of art. In 2005, the High Museum of Art in Atlanta surveyed its extensive collections of nineteenth- and early twentieth-century American decorative arts, deaccessioned a number of objects, and consigned them to auction. This grandiose pitcher, an exuberant expression of the Rococo Revival aesthetic, was included since it was one of a pair and the High retained its mate. The opportunity to introduce a heroic example by Samuel Kirk, the foremost among Baltimore silversmiths, proved auspicious.

Silver
16 3/4 x 9 3/4 x 6 1/4"
(42.5 x 24.8 x 15.9 cm)
Gift of Mrs. James Anderson, Jr.,
and Jas A. Gundry
B.2005.3

96 Asparagus Tongs

1870–75
Gorham Manufacturing Company
(est. 1831)
Providence

Since the 1980s, important examples of flatware have been added to the collection. A spoon by Jeremiah Dummer, the earliest native-born silversmith whose work is known, introduces a survey that spans two centuries, culminating in a group inspired by Egyptian design, and manufactured at a time when modern reforms and the completion of the Suez Canal were bringing Egypt into the family of modern nations. The latter are part of an extensive range of specialized flatware that has been given to the museum by a dedicated group of flatware collectors, Dr. William P. Hood, Jr., Charles and Phyllis Tucker, and Jas A. Gundry—a collection that the museum could not have assembled on its own.

Silver and silver gilt
12 1/4 x 1 5/8 x 1 3/4" (31.1 x 4.1 x 4.4 cm)
Gift of Dr. William P. Hood, Jr.
B.2003.16

BB

97 *Soup Tureen*

1859
Edward Chandler Moore (1827–1891)
for Tiffany & Co. (est. 1837)
New York

Bayou Bend's collection of nineteenth-century silver has grown
exponentially during the last two
decades. Among these accessions
are examples by the triumvirate that
dominated the silver craft and
industry in the nineteenth century:
the partnership of Thomas Fletcher
and Sidney Gardiner (cat. 76); the
Gorham Manufacturing Company
(cats. 94 and 96); and Tiffany & Co.
Tiffany silver is difficult to discern
because, for the first three decades
of its existence, the firm did not
design and make its own pieces but
commissioned them from other
establishments, simply adding its
retailer's mark and then selling them
from its vaunted showrooms. This
classically inspired soup tureen is
inscribed as a bequest from William
Jay, a son of the legendary chief
justice. It bears the mark of the
venerable firm as well as "M" for
Edward C. Moore, the second
generation of a prominent silver-
smithing family who supplied
Tiffany & Co. Less than a decade
later, in 1868, he sold his business
to Tiffany's. Under the terms of
their agreement, Moore stayed on
to oversee design and production.
Under his visionary leadership,
Tiffany & Co. achieved an
international acclaim that no other
American company could approach.

Silver
Tureen: 11 3/4 x 13 1/2 x 9 1/2" (29.8 x 34.3 x 24.1 cm)
Underplate: 3/4 x 13 3/8 x 10 1/4" (1.9 x 34 x 26 cm)
Gift of Colletta and Don F. McMillian
B.97.37.1, .2

98 Hill Country Landscape

1862
Hermann Lungkwitz (1813–1891)
Fredericksburg, Texas

Oil on canvas
18 3/8 x 23 13/16" (46.7 x 60.5 cm)
Gift of Miss Ima Hogg
B.67.39

Unique among institutional centers for American decorative art and paintings, Bayou Bend includes the artistic production of Miss Hogg's native Texas, represented in the Texas Room that was installed in 1961. During the 1960s, Miss Hogg focused her activities on the historic preservation of the village of Winedale, assembling a collection of decorative arts that portrayed the native traditions of German immigrants who had recently fled politically ravaged Germany for the Texas Hill Country. Given her dedication to this new area of collecting, it is no surprise that, when New York dealer Robert Graham offered her in 1967 *Hill Country Landscape* by the German émigré painter Hermann

Lungkwitz, she acted quickly to purchase it. When Lungkwitz left Germany for the United States and Texas, he brought with him a new painterly sophistication and refinement not seen before in Texas. He applied the international romantic tradition of landscape painting to the newly developing and distinctive Texas Hill Country (near San Antonio, its gateway, and Fredericksburg)—with its limestone ledges and caverns, sleepy rivers, and wind-blown cypresses. Like many nineteenth-century American landscapes, this one is a composite, combining recognizable views along the Pedernales and the Guadalupe rivers.
EBN

BB

99 *Music Stand*

1845–60
New Braunfels area, Texas

This specialized furniture form, elegant in its simplicity, is crafted of native walnut and was probably made in the area near New Braunfels, a community in the Texas Hill Country founded by Prince Carl of Solms-Braunfels in March 1845 at the confluence of the Guadalupe and Comal rivers and named for the Solms ancestral castle. Before the year was out, Prince Solms returned to Germany, but the town he left behind prospered as the commercial center for an expanding frontier and, alongside its economic institutions, the community fostered the establishment of its own social and cultural institutions, including sports and musical organizations.

Black walnut
Open: 43 1/4 x 17 7/8 x 19 5/8"
(109.9 x 45.4 x 49.8 cm)
Closed: 43 1/4 x 17 7/8 x 15"
(109.9 x 45.4 x 38.1 cm)
Gift of the William Hill Land & Cattle
Company, in honor of Michael K. Brown
B.2006.2

100 Vase

1918
Newcomb College Pottery (1894–1940),
decorated by Sadie Irvine (1887–1970)
New Orleans

Miss Ima Hogg was unique among
collectors of her generation, and for
that matter, those active since her
time, for cultivating an encyclopedic
view of American art. In her
nineties, she envisioned and began
planning for the Bayou Bend
Collection to extend beyond its
mid-nineteenth-century parameters
to explore some of the later artistic
movements. One that must have
possessed an irresistible attraction
was the pottery produced at the H.
Sophie Newcomb Memorial College,
the women's college of Tulane
University. With the study of this
unique enterprise then nascent,
she engaged her young niece, Alice
Simkins, an alumna of the college
and an art historian, to collaborate
with her on this collecting venture.
When Miss Hogg died a few months
later, Alice persisted in the search
and eventually discovered this iconic
example by Sadie Irvine, the most
illustrious of the Newcomb designers.

Earthenware
11 x 4 1/4" (27.9 x 10.8 cm)
Gift of Alice C. Simkins in honor of
Miss Ima Hogg
B.75.65

MEMBERS OF THE BAYOU BEND COMMITTEE 1960–2006

Mrs. Nancy O'Connor Abendshein**	1998–present
Mrs. Paul Ache, Jr.	1984–86
Mrs. John A. Adkins	1999–2002
Mr. James M. Alexander	1990–91
Mrs. Margaret M. Alkek	2000–05
Mrs. Randolph F. Allen	1999–2000
Mrs. James Anderson, Jr.	1999–present
Mr. Thomas D. Anderson*	1960, 1963–77, 1980–83
Mrs. Thomas D. Anderson	1964–65, 1988–97
Mrs. Thurmon M. Andress	2006–present
Mr. Mark Andrews	1995–98
Mr. Mark Edwin Andrews*	1973–78
Mrs. Harold Armstrong	1994–95
Mr. Isaac Arnold, Jr.	1978–92
Mrs. Isaac Arnold, Jr.	1978–2005
Mrs. Isaac Arnold III	1996–97
Mrs. Robert Arnold	2003–04
Mrs. Edward Babcock	1971–78
Mrs. John S. Bace	1989–90
Mrs. Charles W. Bailey, Jr.	2000–01
Mrs. Floyd Kenneth Bailey	2002–04, 2006–present
Mrs. Ray B. Bailey	1998–2005
Mr. Clayton D. Baird	2005–present
Mrs. Clayton D. Baird	1993–94
Mrs. J. Michael Baldwin	1998–99
Mrs. Rubalee H. Ball	1984
Mr. A. L. Ballard	1997–present
Mrs. John N. Barineau III	2004–05
Mrs. J. Peyton Barnes, Jr.	1986–87
Mrs. Paul F. Barnhart	1977–80
Mrs. Walter M. Bering	1998–99
Mr. James M. Berry	1991–93
Mrs. Edward A. Blackburn, Jr.	1972–73, 1986–89
Mrs. W. Tucker Blaine, Jr.	2005–06

Mrs. Laura Lee Blanton	1985–99
Mrs. Robert S. Bloss	2003–present
Mrs. John F. Bookout, Jr.	1987–2005
Mrs. John F. Bookout III**	1997–present
Mrs. John P. Bornman, Jr.	1995–96
Mr. Alfredo Brener	1990–95
Mrs. Celina Hellmund Brener	1995–present
Mrs. John Brent	1989–91
Mr. Spurgeon K. Britt	1983–93
Mrs. Spurgeon K. Britt	1991–92
Mr. George M. Britton	2000–03
Mr. James L. Britton, Jr.	1978–81
Mr. James L. Britton III	1987–90
Mrs. John J. Britton	2001–02
Mrs. Charles F. Brown	2003–04
Mrs. Randolph Bryan	1960
Mrs. James L. Buaas	2001–02
Ms. Darcie Bundy	1996–2000
Mr. Earl P. Burke, Jr.	1984–85
Mrs. William T. Butler	2003–04
Mr. Dixon H. Cain	1964–74
Mrs. Charles Callery	1963–65
Mrs. Clifford G. Campbell	1988–89, 1992–93
Ms. Catherine Campbell-Hevrdejs	1996–2003
Mr. Paul W. Carlisle, Jr.	2003–05
Mrs. Sanford L. Carr	1991–92
Mrs. Allen H. Carruth	1988–96
Mrs. Marian Catechis	2002–03
Mrs. William H. Caudill	2002–03
Mrs. Jacqueline Baly Chaumette	2005–present
Mr. James Chillman, Jr.	1960
Mrs. James Chillman, Jr.	1960
Mr. Fielding L. Cocke	1998–2001
Mrs. Bobby Smith Cohn	1991–2004
Ms. Jeanie E. Connell	2003–05
Mr. Stephen C. Cook	1989–91
Mrs. Stephen C. Cook	1998–99, 2002–06
Mrs. Theodore Cooper	1971–74

Suggestions for Further Reading

Brown, Michael K. "A Decade of Collecting at Bayou Bend." *Antiques* 128 (September 1985): 514–25.

_____. *The Wilson Potters: An African-American Enterprise in 19th-Century Texas.* Houston: The Museum of Fine Arts, Houston, 2002.

Fox, Stephen. "The Museum of Fine Arts, Houston: An Architectural History, 1924–1986." *The Museum of Fine Arts, Houston, Bulletin*, n.s., XV, nos. 1–2, special bulletin, 1992.

Hart Galleries. *A Very Special Two-Day Auction: An Extensive Collection of Americana, Paintings, Folk Art, Decorations and Objects of Art, Deaccessioned from the Collection of Bayou Bend*, 11–12 April, 1992.

Kirkland, Kate Sayen. "Envisioning a Progressive City: Hogg Family Philanthropy and the Urban Ideal in Houston, Texas, 1910–1975." PhD diss., Rice University, 2004.

Lomax, John A. "Will Hogg, Texan." *Atlantic Monthly* 165 (May 1940): 662–73. Reprint, Austin: University of Texas Press for the Hogg Foundation of Mental Health, 1968.

Marzio, Peter C., et al. *A Permanent Legacy: 150 Works from the Collection of the Museum of Fine Arts, Houston.* Houston: The Museum of Fine Arts, Houston, 1989.

McCarthy, Maura. "50 Years of the *Theta Charity Antiques Show.*" *Theta Charity Antiques Show Catalogue: 50th Anniversary.* Houston, 2002.

The Museum of Fine Arts, Houston. *A Celebration of America's Past: The Theta Charity Antiques Show's Gifts to Bayou Bend.* Houston: The Museum of Fine Arts, Houston, 2002.

Neff, Emily Ballew, with Wynne H. Phelan. *Frederic Remington: The Hogg Brothers Collection of the Museum of Fine Arts, Houston.* Houston: The Museum of Fine Arts, Houston; Princeton: Princeton University Press, 2000.

Sack, Harold, and Max Wilk. *American Treasure Hunt: The Legacy of Israel Sack.* Boston: Little, Brown, and Co., 1986.

Stillinger, Elizabeth. *The Antiquers: The Lives and Careers, the Deals, the Finds, the Collections of the Men and Women Who Were Responsible for the Changing Taste in American Antiques, 1850–1930.* New York: Alfred A. Knopf, 1980.

Warren, David B. "American Decorative Arts in Texas: The Bayou Bend Collection of The Museum of Fine Arts of Houston." *Antiques* 90 (December 1966): 796–815.

_____. "The Empire Style at Bayou Bend: New Period Rooms in Houston." *Antiques* 97 (January 1970): 122–27.

_____. "Recent Acquisitions, The Belter Parlor at Bayou Bend." *The Museum of Fine Arts, Houston Bulletin*, n.s., 2, no. 3, (1971): 30–36.

_____. *Bayou Bend: American Furniture, Paintings and Silver from the Bayou Bend Collection.* Houston: Museum of Fine Arts, Houston; Boston: New York Graphic Society, 1975.

_____. "Ima Hogg, Collector." *Antiques* 121 (January 1982): 228–43.

_____. "The Reopening of Bayou Bend in Houston, Texas." *Antiques* 144 (September 1993): 328–37.

_____. *Bayou Bend Gardens: A Southern Oasis.* Houston: The Museum of Fine Arts, Houston; London: Scala Publishers, 2006.

Warren, David B., Michael K. Brown, Elizabeth Ann Coleman, and Emily Ballew Neff. *American Decorative Arts and Paintings in the Bayou Bend Collection.* Houston: Museum of Fine Arts, Houston; Princeton: Princeton University Press, 1998.

Winchester, Alice, ed. *Collectors and Collections: The Antiques Anniversary Book.* New York: Antiques, 1961.

INDEX

Note: Page numbers in *italics* denote photographs in the essays.
The abbreviation "IH" is for Ima Hogg.